The Generational Algorithm

Rewriting the Emotional Code Passed Down Through Generations

Loading... 0% complete

FRANCISCO CASTILLO

The Generational Algorithm

Rewriting the Emotional Code Passed Down Through Generations

CONTENTS

<AUTHOR_NOTE>

YES, I USED AI (AND NO, I'M NOT HAVING AN IDENTITY CRISIS ABOUT IT)

// README.txt

Plot twist: Your therapist-author needed therapy... from an AI.

After 20 years in the military and a decade as a therapist, I had enough insights to fill a library. Problem was my writing style read like a military field manual had a baby with clinical session notes. Nobody needs to read "The patient exhibited attachment dysregulation secondary to parentification dynamics." Not even other therapists.

Enter AI—my digital writing therapist who never judges me for starting every paragraph with "Research shows..."

Here's what's mine: Every concept, the DECODE method, and yes—the whole "family trauma as social media algorithm" metaphor. That lightning bolt hit me during a session when a client kept checking their phone while describing their toxic family patterns. The connection was so obvious I nearly fell off my therapy chair.

Here's what AI helped with: Making sure you didn't fall asleep by Chapter 2. Translating "therapeutic psychoeducational interventions" into "here's how to stop repeating your dad's mistakes."

Am I smart for using AI? Or does needing AI mean I'm not that smart? Classic overthinking—yes, therapists do it too. We just bill ourselves for it.

Truth is, I wanted to give you the best book possible. Sometimes that means admitting you need a really smart robot to help you sound like a human instead of a walking DSM-5 manual.

(The AI wanted me to end with something more professional. I'm keeping this.)

— Francisco Castillo, LMFT *Human therapist, AI-assisted author, and proof that everyone needs a little help sometimes*

<ABOUT_AUTHOR>

FRANCISCO CASTILLO, LMFT

// User profile loading...

Francisco Castillo is a Licensed Marriage and Family Therapist based in Hawaii who brings a unique blend of military experience, personal transformation, and postmodern therapeutic approaches to his work with individuals and families affected by generational trauma.

Born and raised in Hollister, California, Francisco's path to becoming a therapist was anything but traditional. After struggling academically and leaving high school without graduating, he earned his GED and enlisted in the Navy—at the time, his best chance at building a meaningful adult life. He went on to serve 20 years in active military service, retiring in 2019. While on active duty, Francisco began taking college courses here and there, eventually choosing Psychology as his major and earning his Bachelor of Science in Psychology—all while serving his country. His experiences in the military, combined with his growing understanding of human behavior, deeply influenced his understanding of human resilience, the complexities of relationships, and the profound impact of trauma across generations.

Following his military retirement, Francisco pursued his calling to help others heal, earning his Master of Science in Counseling Psychology from Chaminade University of Honolulu. As a postmodern therapist, he specializes in Internal Family Systems (IFS), narrative therapy, and collaborative approaches that honor each person's unique story and innate wisdom.

Francisco's therapeutic philosophy centers on the belief that people aren't broken—they're running outdated emotional software that can be updated. His work focuses on helping clients identify and transform inherited family patterns, using creative metaphors and contemporary references to make complex psychological concepts accessible and relevant.

His innovative approach to generational healing has helped clients break cycles of trauma and create healthier legacies for future generations. Francisco is particularly passionate about making therapy accessible to communities that have traditionally been underserved or skeptical of mental health support.

When he's not in session or writing, Francisco hosts the podcast "Cruisin' for Clarity with a Therapist," where he explores mental health topics with humor and authenticity. He finds joy in quality time with his family, playing Roblox with his daughter (and losing to her consistently), and listening to his favorite 90s hip-hop artists—the soundtrack to his own transformation journey. (And yes, Tupac over Biggie... always.)

Francisco's personal experience of rewriting his own family algorithm—from high school dropout to respected therapist—infuses his work with authenticity and hope. He knows firsthand that transformation is possible because he's lived it.

The Generational Algorithm was born from his clinical work and his deep commitment to helping people understand that their emotional inheritance doesn't have to be their destiny.

Francisco lives in Hawaii with his family, where the ocean reminds him daily that healing, like waves, comes in cycles—and that even the biggest storms eventually give way to calm seas.

Connect with Francisco:

- Website: https://mhsolutionshawaii.com/
- Podcast: Cruisin' for Clarity with a Therapist
- Instagram: @therapybyfrancisco

Francisco is available for speaking engagements, workshops, and clinical consultation on generational trauma and family systems work.

<INTRODUCTION>
THE NOTIFICATION THAT CHANGED EVERYTHING

//Loading...

5% complete

The notification appeared at 2:47 AM, glowing against Sarah's face in the darkness: "You have memories to look back on today."

Her thumb hovered over it, already knowing what she'd see. Facebook's algorithm had no way of knowing that this particular memory—a family photo from five years ago—was the last one taken before everything changed. Before her brother's overdose. Before her parents' divorce. Before the silence that spread through her family like a virus, infecting every conversation, every gathering, every attempt at connection.

In the photo, they were all smiling. The algorithm saw happiness and thought she'd want to remember. It couldn't detect the vodka on her father's breath, hidden behind his perfect smile. It couldn't measure the weight of her mother's antidepressants, doubled that month but never discussed. It couldn't hear her brother's dealer calling during dinner, the phone buzzing in his pocket as he hugged their grandmother.

Sarah stared at that frozen moment, and something shifted. For the first time, she understood: her family had been running on a faulty algorithm long before Facebook existed. An invisible code, passed down through generations, that determined what could be felt and what must be hidden, what deserved attention and what got deleted, who received love and who got blocked.

Just like she could change her Facebook settings, Sarah wondered: Could she rewrite her family's emotional code?

The Moment Everything Changes

This book exists because of moments like Sarah's—those 2:47 AM revelations when we suddenly see the invisible programming that's been running our lives.

We live in an age where we understand algorithms intimately. We know Instagram learns what we'll double-tap. We recognize when YouTube's recommendations get too specific. We can feel TikTok reading our minds, serving us content we didn't even know we needed.

Yet most of us remain blind to the most powerful algorithm of all—the one our families programmed into us before we could speak, before we could consent, before we even knew we had a choice. Studies show that 75% of adults are unknowingly running emotional software that was programmed before age seven [CS]. By the time you can think about what you're experiencing, your brain is processing 11 million bits of information per second but can only consciously handle about 40 [RS]. Your family's emotional programming determines which 40 make it through.

A Note on Research and Stories in This Book

Statistical Notation Guide: Statistics in this book are marked as follows:

[RS] = Research Study: From peer-reviewed research

[CS] = Clinical Statistic: Based on clinical observations

[IS] = Illustrative Statistic: Representative of patterns

[AS] = Aggregate Statistic: Compiled from multiple sources

This approach allows me to convey important concepts accessibly while being transparent about the source of each claim. My goal is not to present a rigorous academic text, but to offer you practical insights and tools for transformation.

Your Family: The Original Social Network

Long before Mark Zuckerberg dreamed of connecting the world, families were the original social networks. They created echo chambers more powerful than any Facebook could design, filter bubbles that lasted lifetimes, and viral content that spread through DNA and dinner tables.

This emotional algorithm determines everything: which feelings appear in your consciousness and which get automatically filtered, who feels safe to connect with and who triggers your defenses, what behaviors get repeated and what gets blocked, which patterns go viral through generations, how love gets expressed—or doesn't.

But here's what Silicon Valley figured out that our families didn't: algorithms can be updated. Bugs can be fixed. Toxic patterns can be disrupted. The code can be rewritten.

Your Journey Through This Book

Think of this book as a user manual for your emotional operating system—the one you never knew you were running. Through the lens of our digital age, we'll explore:

How your family's algorithm was originally programmed The way trauma goes viral through generations Why you keep scrolling through the same painful patterns Ways to debug your inherited code How your healing can spread exponentially

Throughout this journey, you'll learn to apply a systematic approach I call DECODE—a method for transforming inherited patterns:

Detect your inherited patterns
Examine the source code
Challenge outdated programming
Override with new responses
Download healthier patterns
Evolve your family legacy

This isn't just another acronym to memorize. It's a practical framework you'll use throughout our 90-day transformation, with each chapter building on these six essential steps. By the end of this book, DECODE will become as natural as checking your phone—except this time, you'll be checking and updating the patterns that actually run your life.

Who Needs This Update?

This book is for you if you've ever felt like you're running outdated emotional software—responding to present moments with past programming. It's for you if your family feels like a social media feed you can't unfollow, full of triggers and toxic content. It's for you if you're tired of passing down the same bugs to the next generation.

Your 90-Day Transformation

As you work through this book over the next 90 days, you'll begin to identify the bugs in your emotional programming and install healthier responses that run automatically. This isn't about blaming your family or dwelling in the past. It's about understanding that you're not broken—you're just running outdated software.

A Gentle Warning

As you read this book, you'll uncover family patterns that have been running in the background your entire life. Be gentle with yourself. You're not just reading a book; you're examining code that's been running for generations, created by people doing their best with the programming they inherited.

Your Update Begins Now

Your family installed your first algorithm, but you have administrative access now. You're not just a user anymore—you're the developer.

The notification has appeared. The memory has surfaced. The pattern is visible.

Time to update your emotional algorithm.

… … … // buffering … … …

<CHAPTER_1>
YOUR PERSONALIZED EMOTIONAL FEED //

Loading inherited patterns...

10% complete

Marcus knew something was wrong when he couldn't cry at his father's funeral.

Everyone else was sobbing—his sisters, his aunts, even his stone-faced uncles had tears cutting channels through their weathered faces. But Marcus stood there, dry-eyed, feeling like a robot running a grief.exe program that kept crashing. His chest was a spinning wheel of death, buffering endlessly, unable to load the emotions everyone expected him to display.

His left eye had been twitching for three days. He'd thrown up that morning.

Three months later, he lost it completely in the cereal aisle at Target. Full breakdown over Honey Nut Cheerios—his father's favorite. The tears he couldn't cry at the funeral ambushed him between the granola and instant oatmeal.

"I don't understand," he told his therapist, mortified.

His therapist asked a simple question: "What happened when you cried as a child?"

The memory surfaced in fragments: Marcus, age four, sobbing after falling off his bike. His father's face not concerned but disgusted. "Boys don't cry," he said, his voice carrying the weight of his father's voice, and his father's voice, an echo through generations. "You want to be a little girl?"

In that moment, Marcus's four-year-old brain did what all children's brains do—it adapted for survival. It wrote a program: *tears equal danger, tears equal rejection, tears equal loss of love.* By the time Marcus stood at his father's funeral thirty years later, that program was still running perfectly, blocking every tear before it could form.

Except trauma doesn't follow neat timelines. The tears found their own schedule. A bike commercial. His son's bedtime. Tuesday afternoon for no reason at all.

This is how we all learned to feel—or not feel. Children's brains form over 700 new neural connections per second in the first years of life [RS], each interaction with caregivers literally wiring our emotional circuitry. By age seven, your emotional algorithm is 90% complete [CS]. The software is written, the patterns are set, and most of us spend the rest of our lives running code we don't even know exists.

The Feed That Shapes You

Think about your social media feed for a moment. Within days of joining any platform, the algorithm has figured you out. Your emotional algorithm works exactly the same way, except it started learning the moment you were born.

Dr. Allan Schore, often called the "Einstein of attachment theory," discovered that the right brain—which dominates in early years—doesn't think in words but in feelings, images, and body sensations [RS]. This is why you can't simply think your way out of inherited patterns.

Emma understood this viscerally. She came to therapy because she couldn't figure out why business meetings made her sick. A successful marketing director, confident and accomplished, she would feel her body revolt every time voices rose even slightly in conference rooms.

"It's like my body thinks I'm going to die," she told me, confused by her own reactions.

Together, we traced her body's alarm system to its source. Emma grew up in a house where her parents' fights were weather events—sudden, violent, and impossible to predict. At seven years old, her algorithm had learned: raised voices meant danger, tension meant storm approaching, humor might deflect disaster, staying small meant survival.

Twenty-five years later, in a boardroom in downtown Portland, Emma's body was still running the same storm-survival software she'd written as a seven-year-old. Her emotional feed kept serving her the same content: *danger, danger, danger.* Even when she was safe.

How Patterns Go Viral Through Generations

The cruelest thing about our emotional algorithms is how they spread. Like a TikTok trend that suddenly has everyone doing the same dance, family patterns go viral through generations, each iteration adding its own twist while maintaining the core moves.

The Chen family showed me how trauma compounds across time:

Grandfather Chen survived war through a simple algorithm: *success equals survival, rest equals death.* This code saved his life.

His son inherited the code but amplified it: *success equals worthiness, rest equals laziness.*

Charlotte (third generation) received the most evolved version: *achievement equals bare minimum for existence, rest equals betrayal.*

Charlotte came to therapy at thirty-four, successful by every external measure—Harvard MBA, six-figure salary—and completely hollow inside. She showed me her daily schedule: 5 AM workout, 12-hour workday, evening classes, weekend volunteering. Every moment optimized for productivity.

"When do you rest?" I asked.

She looked at me like I'd asked when she planned to set herself on fire. The virus had evolved. What saved her grandfather was now slowly killing her, but her algorithm couldn't tell the difference.

Understanding and Observing Your Algorithm

Here's what I need you to understand: your emotional algorithm isn't broken. It's doing exactly what it was programmed to do. Every pattern you're frustrated with, every reaction you can't seem to control, every generational curse you're desperate to break—all of it made sense in context. All of it was adaptive when it was written.

Marcus's inability to cry wasn't a flaw—it was a feature that protected him from his father's rejection. Emma's hypervigilance wasn't pathology—it was a brilliant adaptation to an unpredictable environment. Charlotte's relentless productivity wasn't madness—it was loyalty to a family story of survival.

The problem isn't that these algorithms exist. The problem is that we're still running emergency software when the emergency has passed. We're responding to today's relationships with yesterday's programming, creating the very pain we're trying to avoid.

Before you can change your algorithm, you need to see it. This requires developing what I call "witness consciousness"—the ability to observe your patterns while they're running. Like watching your Instagram feed and suddenly noticing, "Wow, the algorithm really thinks I love conspiracy theories about ancient aliens," you need to catch your emotional patterns in action.

Start by noticing what your emotional feed serves you repeatedly: What feelings show up most often? Which emotions never appear? What reactions feel automatic? When do you find yourself in that familiar scroll—the same emotional content, the same relational dynamics, the same inherited patterns playing out again and again?

The moment you see the algorithm is the moment it begins to lose its automatic power. Not all at once—these programs have been running too long for instant deletion. But awareness creates a crack in the code, a moment where you realize: "I'm not choosing this response. It's choosing me." That recognition is where change begins. Every time you catch yourself running inherited code, you create space for choice. You can't debug what you can't see, so awareness itself is the first victory.

Your Seven-Day Algorithm Detection Challenge

This week begins your 90-day transformation journey. Your only job is to **Detect**—the first step in transforming inherited patterns.

Daily Focus:

Day	Activity
Monday	Notice one emotional reaction that feels automatic
Tuesday	Track when you hear your parent's voice coming from your mouth
Wednesday	Identify one "rule" you follow that you never consciously chose
Thursday	Notice your body's response around certain family members
Friday	Catch yourself in one "feed loop"—repeating a familiar pattern
Saturday	Observe which emotions you're allowed to feel vs. forbidden ones
Sunday	Celebrate any moment of awareness, no matter how small

One Key Question to Carry This Week: *"Is this my authentic response, or is this my programming?"*

The Power of Detection

Remember: Detection is powerful. Every time you catch yourself running inherited code, you create space for choice. You can't debug what you can't see, so this week is about seeing clearly.

Start small. Notice without judgment. Observe with curiosity, not criticism. You're not trying to change anything yet—just becoming aware of what's already there.

Recovery Log: Marcus, Day 1

Today I saw my algorithm for the first time. Thirty-seven years of code, running silently in the background. I couldn't cry at my father's funeral because a four-year-old version of me is still protecting us from his disgust. I understand now. The tears aren't gone—they're just archived, waiting for permission to flow. Tomorrow, I practice giving that permission.

Next: Chapter 2 explores how your family's filter determines what you can and cannot see, turning toxic behavior invisible and warping reality to match the family story.

... ... // buffering ... ...

<CHAPTER_2>
FILTERED REALITY //

Applying family perception filters...

18% complete

The dress was blue and black. Science confirmed it, photography experts explained it, and yet millions of people saw white and gold. The 2015 viral phenomenon wasn't about the dress—it was about the discovery that we don't all see the same reality.

Amara learned this when she brought her boyfriend to meet her family. Afterward, in the car, she asked what he thought of dinner.

"Your family seems..." he paused, choosing words carefully, "intense."

"Intense?" Amara was genuinely confused. "They were totally relaxed tonight."

"Your mom criticized everything you ate. Your dad shut down every topic you brought up. Your sister made three comments about your weight."

"That's just how we talk," Amara said, her voice getting defensive. "You don't understand our dynamic."

"I'm just saying what I observed—"

"Well maybe observe less and enjoy more," she snapped. The rest of the ride was silent.

They fought about it for three days. Amara called her sister for validation. "He said you were mean to me. Can you believe that?"

"Sounds like he can't handle a real family," her sister agreed.

But the seed was planted. Over the next months, Amara started noticing things. Then immediately explaining them away. Mom's comment about her job wasn't criticism, it was concern. Dad wasn't shutting her down, he was tired. The weight comments were about health.

She broke up with him two months later. "You made me paranoid about my own family," she accused.

Six months after that, at another family dinner, Amara heard herself making excuses for why she couldn't visit more often. Her mother's response was swift: "I guess we're not important enough."

For the first time, Amara felt something crack. But even then, she pushed the feeling down. It took two more years, a therapist, and countless cycles of seeing-then-denying before she could hold both truths: her family loved her AND their love came wrapped in criticism that had shaped her entire reality.

Even now, in my office, she sometimes says, "But maybe I'm too sensitive. Maybe they're right."

The Installation Process

Family filters don't arrive like Instagram updates with clear notifications. They install slowly, invisibly, one interaction at a time, usually beginning before conscious memory.

The human brain receives 11 million bits of information per second but can only consciously process about 40 bits [RS]. Your family's emotional filters determine which 40 bits make it through—meaning you're literally living in a different reality than someone with different filters. This isn't metaphorical. It's neurological.

Children's brains exist in what neuroscientists call "theta state" until about age seven—the same brainwave state as deep hypnosis [RS]. This means young children are literally in a hypnotic trance, downloading beliefs and filters without critical analysis.

James traced his filter installation to age three. His mother, a surgeon, valued logic above all else. When he fell and scraped his knee, crying, she would say, "Let's be logical about this. Crying doesn't heal wounds."

Young James learned: emotions equal illogical equal worthless. By forty-one, James was a successful engineer whose marriage was failing. His wife would share feelings, and his filter would automatically process them into problems to solve.

"I don't understand," he told me, genuinely bewildered. "I give her solutions to every problem she brings up. Why is she angrier?"

His filter was so efficient he couldn't see that his wife wasn't bringing him problems—she was bringing him feelings.

When Denial Becomes Default

Some filters go beyond distortion—they delete reality entirely. The Patterson family ran industrial-strength denial filters about Dad's drinking. Empty bottles became "recycling day already?" Slurred speech translated to "Dad's just tired." Even a DUI arrest got filtered into a "misunderstanding."

But the filter's true genius was in what it made invisible. Not just the drinking, but the entire emotional ecosystem around it: Mom's hypervigilance, the children's anxiety, the family's isolation.

Their daughter Madison discovered the filter's power at college. Her roommate found her emptying beer bottles from their mini-fridge at 6 AM.

"Party tonight?" the roommate asked.

"No," Madison said, confused. "Just cleaning up."

"Madison... those are my bottles from last month. Why are you cleaning my old beer bottles at dawn?"

Madison's hands were shaking. She'd been unconsciously running her family's algorithm: hide the evidence, maintain the image, protect the secret she didn't even know she was keeping.

How Filters Persist and How to Break Through

Once a filter is installed, it creates a self-reinforcing loop. Nobel Prize-winning psychologist Daniel Kahneman's research shows that it takes ten times more evidence to change a belief than it took to form it [RS]. Your family's filter becomes your brain's shortcut for processing reality. You see what confirms the filter, which strengthens the filter, which shapes what you see. Round and round, until the filter feels like truth and truth feels like lies.

Cultural filters add another layer of reinforcement. Maria grew up in a Mexican-American family where the cultural filter included: family first always, individual needs are selfish, suffering is noble. When Maria started therapy, she couldn't even articulate why she felt guilty for taking time for herself.

"I made myself a cup of tea yesterday," she told me once, "just for me, not for anyone else. And I cried. Over tea. Because it felt so selfish."

The filter marked self-care as selfishness. Maria wasn't just fighting her family's programming—she was up against centuries of cultural code, installed and reinforced by generations of women who survived by serving.

But here's the revolutionary truth: the moment you see the filter is the moment it begins to lose power. Viktor Frankl wrote, "Between stimulus and response there is a space." Your family filter exists in that space, processing stimulus into predetermined response before you even know a choice exists. But once you see the filter, you can expand that space. Create pause between input and output. Give yourself time to ask: Is this reality, or is this the filter?

Lisa practiced expanding this space with her mother. Every phone call followed the same pattern: Mom mentions cousin's achievement, Lisa's filter adds "you're a failure by comparison," Lisa responds defensively. But Lisa learned to pause. To feel the filter activating. To ask herself: What did she actually say?

"Mom said cousin bought house. That's all. The rest—the implied criticism, the comparison—that was the filter adding data that wasn't there."

Without the defensive response, there was no conflict to engage. The filter had been creating battles from neutral data, seeing attacks in observations, hearing criticism in conversation. By catching the filter in action, Lisa could choose whether to respond to what was actually said versus what her programming added. Each time she paused, the space between stimulus and response grew larger, and the filter's automatic power weakened.

Your Seven-Day Filter Awareness Challenge

Week 2 of your 90-day transformation—focuses on **Examining** how your filters operate.

Daily Focus:

Day	Activity
Monday	Notice one automatic interpretation of someone's words
Tuesday	Catch yourself adding meaning that wasn't spoken
Wednesday	Identify a family "truth" that might be filtered
Thursday	Ask someone outside the family how they see a situation
Friday	Practice seeing without interpreting for 5 minutes
Saturday	Notice which realities your family can't discuss
Sunday	Celebrate one moment of seeing clearly

One Key Question to Carry This Week: *"What was actually said versus what did my filter add?"*

The Power of Examination

This week, you're learning to examine the source code of your reactions. When you catch your filter adding meaning, pause and ask:

- What's the raw data here?
- What is my filter adding?
- Where did I learn this interpretation?
- Is it serving me now?

Remember: Examining doesn't mean judging. You're just becoming curious about how your filter operates.

Recovery Log: Amara, Day 47

The filter cracked today. Mom said, "Your sister got promoted" and I waited for the comparison, the criticism, the "why can't you..." But it never came. She was just sharing news. I've been adding subtext that wasn't there for 30 years. How much conflict have I created from neutral data? The world looks different without the family lens. Clearer. Scarier. But real.

Next: Chapter 3 explores how families systematically mute certain emotions, creating "notification settings" that determine which feelings can be expressed and which must remain forever silent.

... ... // buffering ... ...

<CHAPTER_3>

MUTED EMOTIONS //

Checking notification settings...

26% complete

At my daughter's kindergarten graduation, I watched a five-year-old boy's face cycle through pure joy to confusion to carefully constructed blankness in under three seconds. He'd squealed with delight seeing his grandmother, started to run toward her with arms outstretched, then stopped mid-stride. His father's hand on his shoulder wasn't rough, the whispered words weren't harsh, but the message uploaded instantly: "We don't do that here."

The boy returned to his seat, smile replaced with what I call "mute face"—that particular expression children learn when their natural emotions have been marked as spam. By the ceremony's end, he sat perfectly still, perfectly quiet, perfectly muted.

Twenty years later, that boy might sit in an office like mine, successful and empty, saying, "I don't know why I can't feel anything. It's like I'm watching my life through soundproof glass."

The Architecture of Muting

Remember the Mannequin Challenge? Millions froze mid-action, creating eerie tableaus of stillness. That's exactly what emotional muting looks like in families—everyone frozen in acceptable positions, holding their breath, afraid that movement (feeling) will break the spell.

Studies show that suppressing emotions increases physiological stress by 70% and doubles the risk of anxiety and depression [RS - Gross, 2002]. Yet 67% of families have "emotional muting rules"—unspoken agreements about which feelings can't be expressed [CS].

Cindy's family muted through praise. When she was angry: "You're such a good girl for not making a fuss." When she was sad: "So mature, not crying like other kids." Every natural emotion got muted through compliments that taught her: negative feelings make you bad, silence makes you good.

By thirty-four, Cindy was everyone's favorite colleague—never complained, never caused problems, never pushed back. She was also dying inside, her unmuted emotions eating through her stomach lining, attacking her immune system, scrambling her sleep cycles.

"I throw up before big meetings," she told me, ashamed. "My body literally rejects what I'm about to do—sit there and smile while they pass me over for another promotion. But I can't say anything. The words won't come."

What Happens in the Silence

Dr. James Gross at Stanford discovered that emotional suppression doesn't stop emotions—it amplifies them internally. Heart rate increases, blood pressure spikes, stress hormones flood the system [RS]. The body feels MORE while expressing LESS.

Watch how muted emotions manifest:

Muted anger becomes chronic muscle tension, autoimmune disorders, or depression

Muted sadness becomes inexplicable fatigue, compulsive behaviors, or numbness

Muted fear becomes hypervigilance, control issues, or dissociation

The Double Mute and Multiple Layers of Silencing

Some families layer cultural muting on top of family muting, creating what I call the "double mute"—emotions so thoroughly silenced they cease to exist in conscious awareness. Kenji inherited this double mute. Japanese cultural norms said emotional restraint shows maturity. His family amplified this: any emotion shows weakness. By adulthood, his emotional range had compressed to a single note: "fine."

His wife brought him to therapy after finding him on the bathroom floor at 3 AM, sobbing so hard he couldn't breathe. "I don't know what happened," he kept saying. "I'm fine. I'm fine."

But his body had unmuted itself. Twenty years of silenced emotions pouring out in a flood that terrified him. We spent months just learning the language of feelings—teaching him that the tight, hot sensation in his chest had a name: anger. The hollow ache was sadness. The racing thoughts were anxiety. He'd been experiencing these for decades but had no words for them.

The double mute had deleted not just expression but recognition itself. Kenji couldn't express emotions because he literally couldn't identify them. They existed as nameless physical sensations, body memories without language, experiences without categories. Our work began with the basics—emotion wheels, feeling charts, body scans—like teaching a native language that had been forbidden so long it was forgotten.

Unmuting Protocols and Creating New Settings

Unmuting isn't just about expressing suppressed emotions—it's about rebuilding an entire communication system that was disconnected early. The process starts with safety. You can't unmute in the same environment that required muting for survival.

Gabriella learned this when she tried to express frustration at a family dinner. The table went silent. Her father left. "I take it back," Gabriella said quickly. "Everything's fine." The family algorithm had detected unauthorized emotion and initiated emergency shutdown.

So we started smaller. Gabriella practiced unmuting in her journal first—private, no consequences. Then in therapy—professional container. Then with her support group—others unmuting too. Then with a trusted friend—chosen family. Each space let her raise the volume slightly. Whisper became speaking voice became full expression.

When you start unmuting, expect an "extinction burst"—your internal algorithm panicking because you're violating core programming. Isabella experienced this after expressing mild frustration to her mother. Her anxiety skyrocketed: "She'll never speak to me again. I'm a terrible daughter." We sat with it. Let the alarm bells ring. Waited for the system to realize she had expressed frustration and the world hadn't ended.

But you don't have to unmute everything, everywhere, all at once. Like customizing phone notifications, you can choose what emotions get full volume with safe people, what stays on vibrate in professional settings, what remains muted with unsafe family members. The goal isn't to become an emotional broadcaster, sharing every feeling with everyone. It's to have choice—to consciously decide what to express where, rather than running an outdated algorithm that mutes everything automatically.

Daniel created what he called his "emotional notification matrix":

- With his therapist: All emotions, full volume
- With his partner: Most emotions, clear expression
- With close friends: Selective sharing, authentic but boundaries
- With work colleagues: Professional emotions only
- With family of origin: Carefully chosen moments
- With toxic father: Maintained mute for safety

This wasn't repression—it was conscious choice. The difference between can't express and choosing not to. Between muted by fear and silent by wisdom.

Your Seven-Day Unmuting Challenge

Week 3 of your 90-day transformation—is about **Challenging** the mute programming.

Daily Focus:

Day	Activity
Monday	Write one muted feeling in your journal
Tuesday	Tell someone "I feel..." without editing
Wednesday	Let your body express an emotion (movement, sound)
Thursday	Practice saying "no" to something small
Friday	Share a difficult emotion with someone safe
Saturday	Notice the urge to mute and don't
Sunday	Celebrate using your emotional voice

One Key Question to Carry This Week: *"What would I express if I knew it was safe?"*

The Power of Challenging

This week, challenge your mute button by:

- Questioning who benefits from your silence
- Testing if expressing emotions is actually dangerous now
- Noticing the gap between predicted catastrophe and actual outcome
- Building evidence that emotions are survivable

Remember: Start small. Your system needs proof that unmuting is safe.

Recovery Log: Cindy, Day 89

Told my boss I was disappointed about the promotion today. My body prepared for death—heart racing, stomach churning, hands shaking. But I said it anyway. He looked surprised but not angry. Said he understood and we'd talk about next steps. I didn't die. I didn't get fired. I used my voice, and the world kept spinning. Thirty-four years old and I'm just learning to speak.

Next: Chapter 4 examines how families create complex access systems—who gets let in, who gets blocked, and why we often have stricter boundaries with spam callers than with toxic relatives.

… … … // buffering … … …

<CHAPTER_4>
BLOCKED AND UNFRIENDED //

Scanning access permissions...

34% complete

The notification arrived at Rachel's therapy session: "Mom is requesting to follow you on Instagram."

Rachel stared at her phone, then at me, then back at her phone. Her mother—who had spent forty years criticizing every aspect of Rachel's existence—wanted access to her carefully curated digital space.

"I have to accept, right?" Rachel's voice was small. "She's my mother."

"Do you let everyone follow you?" I asked.

"No, of course not. I'm careful about who—" She stopped. The realization dawned slowly. "Oh my god. I have stricter boundaries with strangers on the internet than with the person who hurts me most."

She moved to decline the request. Her finger hovered. Moved away. "But what if she asks why? What if she sees I'm active but haven't accepted? What if—"

That afternoon, Rachel accepted the request.

She texted me at 11 PM: "She commented on three photos. My apartment's 'depressing.' I feel sick."

Rachel blocked her mother at 2 AM. Unblocked her by 6 AM after panic texts about chest pains.

For three months, the pattern repeated: Block after cruel comments. Unblock after guilt trips. Restrict stories. Mom notices, cries. Unrestrict. Try muting. Check anyway. Currently: limited profile, comments off, changes weekly.

"I know I should just block her completely," Rachel said, exhausted. She'd checked her mother's profile 47 times this week. "But I can't. Not yet. Maybe not ever. Is that pathetic?"

"It's human," I replied.

She still adjusts settings obsessively. Still gets Sunday migraines—her mother's scrolling day. Six months later, she's found a middle ground that shifts constantly: some posts visible, others hidden, boundaries that flex and tighten like breathing.

Progress isn't always a straight line.

The Family Access Algorithm

We live in an age where everyone understands digital boundaries. We block spam, report harassment, restrict stories, limit comments. Yet when it comes to family, we hand over all-access passes to people who wouldn't pass the most basic follower screening.

73% of adults report feeling obligated to maintain contact with damaging family members [CS]. We block spam calls instantly but give unlimited access to people who consistently harm our mental health. It's like jumping out of moving cars for viral fame while ignoring obvious safety risks.

The family algorithm tells us that DNA is a VIP pass to your life. But what if blood relation didn't automatically grant backstage passes? What if "family" was a role earned through respect, not an all-access badge granted by genetics?

The Spectrum of Boundaries

Not every difficult relationship requires the nuclear option. Like social media platforms offer various restriction levels, you can customize family access to match their impact on your wellbeing.

Katie discovered the power of the "snooze" function during her pregnancy. Her mother's anxiety was contaminating every moment: "Are you eating enough?" "That's too much exercise." "My friend's daughter had complications..."

Katie implemented a communication break: "Mom, I'll update you monthly during pregnancy. I need this time to connect with my body and baby without outside input."

Her mother protested, but Katie held firm. The break gave her space to experience pregnancy on her own terms.

Daniel mastered restricted access with his critical father. Complete blocking felt impossible—they worked in the same industry. So he created boundaries: professional events only, public spaces only, time limits enforced, topics pre-approved, support person present.

"It's like putting parental controls on a parent," Daniel explained. "I decide what content he can access, when, and for how long."

When Full Blocking is Necessary and Managing the Aftermath

Some relationships are too toxic for half-measures. Like blocking someone spreading revenge porn or death threats, sometimes family members require complete removal from your life.

Sophia made this choice after her mother's thirteenth violation of clearly stated boundaries—showing up at work uninvited, calling her boss, posting private struggles on Facebook, attempting to break up her marriage.

"But she's your mother," people said.

"Exactly," Sophia replied. "She had more power to harm me than anyone. That's why the block is permanent."

When you change access settings—whether it's a full block or just new boundaries—expect your family's algorithm to glitch. Hard. Like an app sending increasingly desperate notifications when you try to delete it, family systems panic when members assert boundaries. This is what psychologists call an "extinction burst"—the pattern fighting for its life.

Not every boundary violation requires Sophia's nuclear option. Sometimes the breach is smaller—a mother who can't respect that her adult daughter needs basic privacy, a father who won't stop offering unsolicited advice, a sibling who treats your home like theirs. But even these "simple" boundaries can trigger spectacular meltdowns.

Jessica documented her mother's extinction burst after implementing basic boundaries. The pattern was predictable: seventeen calls on day one, email to husband by day three, Facebook drama by day five, mysterious health emergency by day seven, siblings recruited by day ten, workplace ambush by day fourteen.

"It was like watching a toddler tantrum in slow motion," Jessica said. "If I'd given in at any point, I'd have taught her that harassment works."

She held steady. Documented everything. Maintained the boundary. Eventually, the extinction burst exhausted itself. Her mother learned the new rules: respect boundaries or lose access. The key was understanding that the size of the tantrum often matches the importance of the boundary. The more necessary the boundary, the harder the system fights against it.

Navigating Guilt and Creating Your New Access System

The hardest part of boundaries isn't setting them—it's managing the internal guilt algorithm that activates when you do. This guilt isn't random. It's programmed by the same system that benefits from your lack of boundaries.

Antonio's Portuguese family's algorithm included heavy guilt coding: "Família é tudo"—Family is everything. Setting boundaries with his gambling-addicted brother felt like betraying heritage, culture, God himself.

But Antonio learned to debug the guilt: Is this proportionate? Whose voice is speaking? What would I tell a friend? Is this based on current reality?

"The guilt is just an error message," he realized. "Old algorithm warning me I'm violating defunct code. I can acknowledge it without obeying it."

You are the administrator of your own life. You get to decide who enters your space and under what conditions. Start by auditing current access levels. Who has unlimited access? What damage does it cause? Which boundaries would increase wellbeing? Then create new settings:

Full access for people who respect boundaries and nourish you—those who've earned deep trust through consistent respect. **Restricted access** for difficult but necessary relationships—people working on change, situational connections, professional obligations. **Blocked** for active abusers and boundary violators—those toxic beyond repair, dangerous to your wellbeing.

Remember: These settings aren't permanent. Someone blocked today might earn restricted access through genuine change. Someone with full access might require restriction after boundary violations. You can adjust as situations evolve.

After the extinction burst, after the guilt waves, after the family system recalibrates to your new settings—peace arrives. Not the false peace of compliance, but the real peace of protected space. Vanessa described it perfectly six months after blocking her narcissistic father:

"I wake up without dread. My phone is just a phone, not a portal for abuse. My home feels safe because she can't enter it. My thoughts are my own because she can't insert herself. I didn't know life could be this quiet. This mine."

Your Seven-Day Boundary Installation Challenge

Week 4 of your 90-day transformation—focuses on **Override**: implementing new access controls.

Daily Focus:

Day	Task
Monday	List who has unlimited access to your life
Tuesday	Identify one boundary you need to set
Wednesday	Practice saying it out loud (alone first)
Thursday	Implement one small boundary
Friday	Hold steady through any pushback
Saturday	Document responses for patterns
Sunday	Celebrate maintaining your boundary

One Key Question to Carry This Week: *"Is this person's access to me earned or assumed?"*

The Power of Override

This week, override old programming by:

- Acting opposite to guilt's demands
- Implementing boundaries despite discomfort
- Choosing your wellbeing over others' comfort
- Building evidence that boundaries improve relationships

Remember: The size of the tantrum often matches the importance of the boundary.

Recovery Log: Sophia, Day 189

Blocked my mother today. Hardest thing I've ever done. Twenty years of trying to earn love from someone incapable of giving it. The extinction burst is epic—flying monkeys deployed, guilt bombs dropping. But my therapist reminded me: "The size of the tantrum matches the importance of the boundary." My nervous system is already celebrating. For the first time, I feel safe in my own existence.

Next: Chapter 5 reveals how family roles get reversed—when children become parents and parents become children—and why breaking free from parentification is essential for authentic adulthood.

... ... // buffering ... ...

<CHAPTER_5>
FLIP THE SWITCH //

Reversing role assignments...

42% complete

The "Flip the Switch" TikTok challenge had parents and kids swapping roles for laughs—dad in daughter's crop top, teen in father's suit. But for parentified children, this isn't a 15-second video. It's their entire childhood, wearing responsibilities that don't fit, performing roles they never auditioned for, with no one filming the struggle.

I watched eight-year-old Jamie demonstrate this at a community health fair. Her mother's blood sugar dropped—a frequent occurrence with poorly managed diabetes. While other children played in the bounce house, Jamie was already moving with practiced efficiency. She retrieved glucose tablets from her mother's purse, checked the expiration date, counted out the correct dose, and guided her mother to a chair.

"It's okay, Mommy," she said in a voice too steady for eight years old. "Remember, we wait fifteen minutes then check again. I'll time it."

A nurse approached to help, but Jamie waved her off. "We've got this. Right, Mom?"

The other parents watched with admiration. "So mature!" they said. "What a little helper!" They saw responsibility. I saw theft—a childhood stolen in plain sight.

The Invisible Promotion and Its Consequences

One in seven children become parentified—forced into adult roles before age 18 [AS]. These children are three times more likely to develop anxiety disorders, five times more likely to struggle with boundaries, and carry a 70% higher caregiver burden throughout life [CS].

Parentification doesn't announce itself with fanfare. The promotion happens quietly, desperately, one impossible responsibility at a time. Dr. Bruce Perry's research shows that children forced into caretaking roles develop overdeveloped stress response systems and underdeveloped play/creativity centers [RS]. Their brains literally reshape around hypervigilance and responsibility.

Kelly discovered how deep her programming ran when she found herself lecturing her therapist about proper nutrition. Forty-three years old, successful physician, and she was explaining the food pyramid like her therapist was a child who needed guidance.

"I'm doing it again, aren't I?" she said, catching herself mid-explanation.

We traced it back. Seven-year-old Kelly, making grocery lists because Mom was too depressed to shop. Eight-year-old Kelly, cooking dinner for younger siblings. Nine-year-old Kelly, budgeting household money, calling utility companies in her most grown-up voice.

"I had a whole script," she remembered. "'This is Mrs. Simmons. I need to discuss our account.' They never questioned it. A child playing adult so convincingly that the world went along with it."

Two Types of Theft: Instrumental and Emotional

Parentification comes in two forms, both damaging in unique ways.

Instrumental Parentification involves physical caretaking—cooking, cleaning, managing finances, caring for siblings. The child becomes the family's operational manager. They learn to read expiration dates before they can read chapter books, balance checkbooks before they balance on bicycles, care for others before they learn to care for themselves.

Emotional Parentification requires managing parents' feelings—being their confidant, mediating conflicts, providing emotional support. The child becomes the family's therapist. They learn to decode adult emotions before understanding their own, carry secrets too heavy for their shoulders, provide comfort when they need comforting.

David experienced both. His system crash came at thirty-seven. Successful lawyer, perfect father, model citizen—until the day he couldn't get out of bed.

"I've been tired since I was nine," he told me.

Nine. When his father left and his mother crumbled. When David became the man of the house by default. His childhood job description included everything from emotional regulation for his unstable mother to financial planning with paper route money to parenting younger siblings. No needs allowed. No burden permitted. No childhood possible.

Here's the complicated truth: parentified children develop remarkable abilities. They become hypercompetent, deeply empathetic, incredibly responsible. These aren't gifts—they're survival adaptations. But they feel like superpowers, and the world rewards them accordingly.

"I'm everyone's favorite employee, worst intimate partner," David explained. "I can save your company but not let you love me. I can manage crisis but not receive care. I can solve problems but not share vulnerability."

The adaptation that saved him as a child was killing his adult relationships. The very skills that made him indispensable made him untouchable. He could give endlessly but couldn't receive. He could support others but couldn't lean on anyone. He could be everyone's rock but no one's soft place to land.

Flipping the Switch Back and Breaking the Inheritance

The beautiful lie parentification tells is that the switch can't flip back. That once you've been the adult, you can't reclaim childhood. But switches are designed to flip both ways.

Carmen discovered this at a children's birthday party. She was organizing games, managing toddlers, solving parent dramas—her usual role—when the hired clown pulled her into a silly dance.

"I can't," she said automatically. "I need to—"

"You need to be silly," the clown said. "Doctor's orders."

Carmen found herself dancing. Badly. Ridiculously. Like a child. For three minutes, she wasn't managing anything. She cried the entire drive home.

"I couldn't remember the last time I did something just for fun," she said. "Not productive fun. Just stupid, silly, purposeless fun."

You can't go back and have the childhood you missed. But you can give yourself what psychologists call "corrective experiences"—new moments that heal old wounds. You become your own good-enough parent, providing what was missing.

The cruelest aspect of parentification is its generational reach. Parentified children often parentify their own children—not from malice, but because they don't know relationships can work differently. The cycle continues until someone consciously breaks it.

Anthony caught himself mid-flip. His six-year-old daughter was patting his back, saying, "It's okay, Daddy. I'll help you feel better." The exact words he'd said to his mother at that age.

"And I was letting her," he told me, horrified. "I was downloading my programming straight into her system."

That recognition changed everything. Anthony began consciously modeling healthy adult-child dynamics—handling his emotions himself, letting his daughter be comforted instead of comforting, protecting her from adult problems.

"Yesterday she threw a tantrum about socks," he said proudly. "Just lost it over socks being the wrong color. And I let her be six. Let her be unreasonable. It was beautiful."

He was giving his daughter what he never had—permission to be a child. Permission to need without providing. Permission to feel without fixing. Every time he maintained appropriate roles, he rewrote generational code.

Your Seven-Day Switch-Flipping Challenge

Week 5 of your 90-day transformation—focuses on **Downloading** healthier patterns.

Daily Focus:

Day	Activity
Monday	Do one thing just for fun (no productivity allowed)
Tuesday	Ask someone else to handle something you'd normally do
Wednesday	Express a need without immediately meeting others' needs
Thursday	Play for 15 minutes (games, coloring, anything childlike)
Friday	Let someone take care of you in a small way
Saturday	Say "I don't know" when asked to solve a problem
Sunday	Celebrate not being responsible for everything

One Key Question to Carry This Week: *"Am I responding as an adult, or as the parentified child I once was?"*

The Power of Download

This week, download new patterns by:

- Practicing age-appropriate responses repeatedly
- Building new neural pathways through play
- Creating evidence that you can receive care

- Installing boundaries between adult and child roles

Remember: You're learning to be the adult to yourself that you needed as a child.

Recovery Log: Anthony, Day 342

Bought finger paints today. Spent an hour making terrible art. No purpose. No product. Just me, colors, and mess. Mom would have made me clean up immediately, find a purpose, make it useful. But I just sat there, forty-five years old, with purple paint on my nose, being useless. Being childish. Being free. The switch is flipping back.

Next: Chapter 6 explores how your earliest relationships create an invisible algorithm for all future connections—why you're magnetically drawn to certain people and allergic to others.

… … … // buffering … … …

<CHAPTER_6>

FOLLOW, UNFOLLOW //

Analyzing attachment protocols...

50% complete

Remember when Instagram's algorithm got so good it started showing you ads for things you only thought about? That's your attachment system—predicting and pursuing relationships before your conscious mind even realizes what's happening. You're following a script written before you could read.

Raul thought he was having a stroke. Heart racing, vision blurring, hands shaking—all because his girlfriend hadn't responded to his text in three hours. At thirty-four, a successful architect with two degrees, he was hiding in his office bathroom, refreshing his phone obsessively, convinced that silence meant abandonment.

His girlfriend had been in a meeting. But when she finally texted back, her message was tense: "Raul, we need to talk about this. Again."

That night, she laid it out: "I can't have my phone on me 24/7. Your panic when I don't immediately respond is suffocating me."

"I'm working on it," Raul promised, the same promise he'd made last month.

"You said you'd go to therapy."

"I will. I just need to find the right person."

She looked tired. "I love you, but I can't be responsible for regulating your attachment system. It's exhausting."

They'd had this fight four times now. Each time, Raul promised change. Each time, he'd do better for a week, maybe two, before the panic returned. He'd just hide it better—checking her social media activity instead of texting, driving by her office to see if her car was there, creating elaborate mental stories about why she must be pulling away.

Two months later, she ended it. "I can't be your emotional regulation system anymore. You need to work on this."

Raul spent the next year in therapy, slowly understanding how his mother's postpartum depression had wired him for abandonment fear. Even with insight, dating remained brutal. He'd match with someone on an app, and the cycle would begin:

First date going well → They text the next day → Relief → They take four hours to respond → Panic spiral → Second date → They seem interested → Temporary calm → They're busy one weekend → Convinced it's over → Third date → Getting closer → Terror increases

"I'm aware I'm doing it," Raul told his therapist. "I watch myself becoming clingy and desperate, but I can't stop. It's like watching a car crash in slow motion."

The Algorithm of Connection: Your Relationship Operating System

Attachment patterns form in the first 18 months of life and predict relationship outcomes with 75% accuracy fifty years later [RS]. You're running love software programmed before you could walk. 85% of adults unconsciously recreate their childhood attachment pattern in every significant relationship [AS].

Think of attachment styles as operating systems for relationships:

Secure Attachment (50%): These fortunate individuals had consistently responsive caregivers. They're comfortable with intimacy and independence, trust others, communicate directly.

Hannah demonstrated this beautifully. When her partner needed space after an argument, she felt the sting but thought, "He needs time to process. We'll talk when he's ready." No panic. No chase. Just regulated acceptance.

Anxious Attachment (20%): Like Raul, they constantly monitor relationship status, need excessive reassurance, fear abandonment intensely. They're following everyone who might leave, terrified of being unfollowed.

Avoidant Attachment (25%): These individuals maintain emotional distance, value hyper-independence, dismiss attachment needs. Derek kept his girlfriend of three years at careful arm's length—separate apartments, limited disclosure. "I love her," he insisted, "I just need space."

Disorganized Attachment (5%): They run approach-avoid patterns, desperately seeking closeness while fearing it. Anaya described it perfectly: "I pull people close then push them away. It's like having two different operating systems fighting for control."

Following Ghosts: The Magnetic Pull of Familiar Pain

Dr. Amir Levine's studies show that anxiously attached individuals literally have heightened attraction to avoidant partners—the very people most likely to trigger their abandonment fears [RS]. We unconsciously select partners who confirm our attachment expectations.

Elena's dating history read like a casting call for the same role: emotionally unavailable musician, workaholic who "needed space," married man who couldn't commit.

"Why do I keep choosing men who can't be there for me?" she asked.

Because her attachment algorithm was programmed by a father who traveled constantly. Love meant longing. Presence meant temporary. She was following ghosts, pursuing absence, swiping right on abandonment.

She tried dating someone available once. Lasted three weeks. "He texted too much," she explained. "Felt suffocating." She was already swiping again, searching for familiar distance.

When someone with anxious attachment gets "unfollowed"—broken up with, ghosted—their system doesn't just hurt; it crashes. Studies show the same brain regions activate during rejection as during physical pain [RS]. The metaphor becomes literal: disconnection wounds.

Raul discovered this when his ex-blocked him on everything after their breakup. The digital severing sent him into full system failure—

couldn't eat, couldn't sleep, couldn't work. He created fake accounts to monitor her.

"It's pathetic," he said. "But I literally can't stop. It's like my brain needs to know she still exists."

His attachment system, programmed for hypervigilance, couldn't compute the sudden absence. Adult knowledge that he'd survive was overridden by infant programming that said disconnection meant death. The ghost he was following had vanished, and his entire system went into panic mode searching for it.

Updating Your Attachment Algorithm: The Path to Earned Security

The beautiful truth: attachment is neuroplastic. Your brain remains capable of forming new pathways. What psychologists call "earned secure attachment" is possible through consistent practice and safe relationships.

Oprah Winfrey openly discusses transforming from disorganized attachment to earned secure: "I had to learn that love wasn't supposed to hurt, that consistency wasn't boring, that safety wasn't a trap."

The update process requires both insight and practice. Understanding your attachment style intellectually is step one. Repeatedly choosing different responses—despite every alarm bell in your system—is where real change happens.

Elena broke her pattern through deliberate rewiring. She almost swiped left on her now-partner because he seemed "too nice." That's when she realized nice felt foreign because available felt wrong.

"Every consistent text felt suspicious," she recalled. "Every reliable plan felt like a trap. It took months to realize he's just actually here. Available. Present. My system kept waiting for the other shoe to drop, for him to disappear like Dad always did. The shoe never dropped. Eventually, I stopped flinching."

The update wasn't instant. Elena had to override her algorithm's warnings hundreds of times. Each consistent interaction was a small patch in her code. Each moment of choosing to trust despite her programming was a step toward earned security.

Your Seven-Day Attachment Awareness Challenge

Week 6 of your 90-day transformation—focuses on **Evolving** your attachment patterns.

Daily Focus:

Day	Practice
Monday	Notice one moment of attachment activation
Tuesday	Identify whose love you're still seeking
Wednesday	Practice sitting with connection discomfort
Thursday	Do opposite of attachment impulse once
Friday	Share appropriate vulnerability with someone
Saturday	Notice who you follow/avoid and why
Sunday	Celebrate any moment of secure behavior

One Key Question to Carry This Week: *"Is this how I truly want to connect, or is this my attachment pattern choosing for me?"*

The Power of Evolve

This week, evolve your patterns by:

- Modeling secure behaviors for others
- Creating ripples in your relationship network
- Building evidence that new patterns work
- Passing healthier attachment to next generation

Remember: You can't delete your attachment style, but you can evolve it through practice.

Recovery Log: Elena, Day 237

Finally understood why I date ghosts. Every unavailable partner was my father in different clothing. I wasn't seeking love—I was seeking the familiar ache of almost-but-not-quite. Today I swiped right on someone available. My whole system screamed "boring!" That's how I knew I was on the right track.

Next: Chapter 7 reveals how some relationships create neurological addiction—why you return to people who hurt you, unable to stop despite clear damage.

… … … // buffering … … …

<CHAPTER_7>
STUCK IN THE LOOP //

Breaking cycle detected...

58% complete

Remember the Cinnamon Challenge? Millions voluntarily tortured themselves for views, repeating harmful behavior despite obvious pain. Trauma bonds work identically—we return to relationships that hurt us, unable to stop despite clear damage, performing pain for an audience of one who'll never truly applaud.

Sophia checked who viewed her story for the forty-seventh time that day. Jordan had watched it six hours ago, but still hadn't responded to her text from yesterday. The last time this happened, he disappeared for a week, then showed up at 2 AM with flowers and tears, swearing he'd changed.

She knew the pattern: idealization for 48-72 hours, growing coldness, sudden disappearance, dramatic return with promises, endless repeat.

"I know it's toxic," she told me, hands shaking as she checked her phone again. "I know about trauma bonding. But knowing doesn't stop the craving."

Because trauma bonds aren't logical—they're neurological. People in trauma bonds check their phones 147 times daily—three times more than average users [AS]. The intermittent reinforcement of toxic relationships creates stronger neural addiction patterns than consistent love [RS]. Your brain literally becomes hooked on dysfunction.

The Neuroscience of Addiction: When Love Becomes a Drug

Dr. Patrick Carnes found that betrayal bonds create actual changes in brain structure [RS]. The regions responsible for critical thinking literally shrink while emotional centers become hyperactive. You can't think your way out because you're thinking center is offline.

Sandra's brain on Jordan looked like an addiction scan: decreased prefrontal cortex activity, hyperactivated amygdala, hijacked reward system, exhausted stress response.

"It's like my smart brain goes offline around him," she explained. "I run a successful business, make important decisions every day. But with Jordan, I become someone I don't recognize."

The trauma bond had literally rewired her neural pathways. Every cycle of abuse-reconciliation strengthened the connection, like a path worn deeper with each pass. Trauma bonding activates the same brain regions as gambling addiction [RS]. The unpredictable rewards—moments of kindness amid abuse—create a more powerful psychological hook than consistent positive treatment.

Jake explained it perfectly: "My ex would disappear for days, maybe cheating, then return with desperate passion. The makeup sex was incredible. Now I'm with someone consistent, kind, reliable—and I feel nothing."

His heart wasn't broken. His neural pathways were. They'd learned that love equals uncertainty plus fear plus occasional reward. Steady love didn't compute. Like a gambler at a slot machine, he'd become addicted not to winning but to the possibility of winning—not to love but to the chance of love.

The Generational Loop: Trauma Bonds Through Time

We don't just trauma bond with romantic partners. Often, the original trauma bond is with a parent—the first person who taught us that love comes with conditions, that care is unpredictable, that we must earn what should be freely given.

Christopher traced his pattern through three generations like a detective following evidence. Grandmother stayed with alcoholic grandfather "for the children." Mother married three addicts, always finding projects to fix. Christopher was attracted exclusively to "broken birds who need saving." Now his twelve-year-old daughter was already trying to fix troubled friends.

"I watched my daughter give her lunch money to a 'friend' who constantly bullied her," Christopher said. "She said, 'But sometimes she's nice to me.' That's when I realized—I taught her this. Three generations of confusing crumbs with love."

In the digital age, these patterns have new venues. Social media has weaponized trauma bonding. Love bombing happens via excessive texts—200 messages one day, silence the next. Devaluation occurs through strategic silence—reading messages without responding, viewing stories without interaction. Surveillance continues through digital breadcrumbs—likes without communication, follows without connection.

Sandra's trauma bond with Jordan played out entirely through phones. Two hundred texts on good days, complete silence on bad days. Obsessive story monitoring. Reading into every emoji. Panic at delayed responses.

"I was trauma bonded to a notification pattern," she realized. "His attention was my drug, and he controlled the supply through his phone. We had our entire relationship through screens—the perfect medium for intermittent reinforcement."

Breaking the Loop: The Neuroscience of Freedom

Selena Gomez publicly discussed breaking her trauma bond pattern: "I kept choosing the same type of person in different bodies. Therapy helped me see I was addicted to the push-pull, not the person. Breaking that pattern was harder than any physical detox."

Breaking trauma bonds requires full-system intervention because you're literally going through withdrawal. Just like substance detox, it creates actual symptoms: physical pain, obsessive thoughts, sleep disruption, intense cravings. Your brain, deprived of its chaos drug, rebels.

Sandra implemented what she called a "neural detox protocol":

- **No contact:** Blocked Jordan on everything
- **Accountability:** Best friend held her phone at night
- **Replacement behaviors:** Ran when urges hit
- **Support system:** Joined a trauma bond recovery group
- **Documentation:** Kept a reality check list of his harmful behaviors

"Day 23 was hell," Sandra recalled. "I literally felt like I was dying. My body was convinced breaking the bond meant death. But Day 24 was slightly better. Day 50, I laughed without him. Day 90, I couldn't imagine going back."

Your Seven-Day Trauma Bond Break Challenge

Week 7 of your 90-day transformation—focuses on **Detecting** toxic cycles (beginning our second DECODE cycle).

Daily Focus:

Day	Action
Monday	Map your relationship cycles
Tuesday	Identify the intermittent rewards keeping you hooked
Wednesday	Create your Reality Check Document
Thursday	Practice one day of no checking
Friday	Tell someone about the pattern
Saturday	Feel the discomfort without acting
Sunday	Celebrate any broken cycle moment

One Key Question to Carry This Week: *"Am I addicted to this person, or to the cycle of pain and relief?"*

The Power of Detection (Round Two)

Now you're detecting at a deeper level:

- Noticing not just patterns but addictive cycles
- Seeing how intermittent reinforcement hooks you
- Recognizing trauma bonds versus real love
- Identifying generational transmission of these patterns

Remember: The size of the withdrawal confirms the strength of the trauma bond.

Recovery Log: Sandra, Day 90

Three months no contact. The withdrawal was real—throwing up, not sleeping, convinced I'd die without him. But somewhere around day 60, the fog lifted. I saw it clearly: I wasn't addicted to him. I was addicted to the cycle. To the slot machine of his attention. Today someone asked me out—someone consistent, kind, present. My trauma bond brain called it "boring." That's when I knew I should say yes.

Next: Chapter 8 uncovers how family secrets shape behavior across generations—the hidden truths that influence everything while remaining carefully buried.

... ... // buffering ... ...

<CHAPTER_8>
THE ARCHIVE OF SECRETS //

Accessing hidden files...

66% complete

#ThrowbackThursday has people posting old photos, unaware they're sharing carefully curated lies. That "perfect family Christmas 1987" hides Dad's affair, Mom's pills, Sister's pregnancy. We archive the truth and display the fiction, then wonder why nothing feels real.

Nathan's mother had one photo album she kept in her closet, separate from the others. As children, Nathan and his siblings knew not to ask about it. Even at forty-three, helping his mother move to assisted living, Nathan felt his handshake reaching for that album.

Inside: photos of a baby. Not him. Not his sisters. A baby that looked exactly like him at that age.

"Thomas," his mother said quietly. "Your brother. Born before you. Lived three days."

Forty-three years of family life, and Nathan had never known he had a brother. But suddenly, everything made sense. His mother's overprotection. The way she cried every May 15th. Her panic when he played sports. The empty chair energy at every gathering.

"We all felt him," Nathan told me later. "This ghost brother we didn't know existed. He was archived, but he shaped everything."

96% of families have at least one significant secret affecting multiple generations [IS]. These hidden truths alter family dynamics for an average of 47 years after the secret is created [CS].

The Architecture of Secrets

Family secrets create what researchers call "toxic knowledge"—information that exists in the system but can't be acknowledged [RS]. Dr. Bessel van der Kolk's brain imaging research shows that keeping secrets activates the same neural networks as physical pain [RS]. The phrase 'painful secrets' is neurologically literal—your brain processes hidden truth as injury.

Family secrets organize themselves into predictable categories:

The Shame Archives contain addiction histories, mental illness, criminal behavior, financial ruin, sexual abuse. These secrets carry the message: "This makes us bad people."

The Betrayal Files hold affairs and illegitimate children, hidden marriages or divorces, adoption truths, paternity questions, family exile reasons. The core belief: "Trust would destroy us."

The Loss Folders store miscarriages and stillbirths, suicides rewritten as accidents, disappeared family members, given-up children, deaths by stigmatized causes. The underlying fear: "We can't survive the truth of our losses."

The Identity Encryption hides ethnicities or race, concealed religion, sexuality or gender truths, name changes, immigration lies. The driving force: "Our real selves aren't acceptable."

Brenda discovered her family's archive when DNA testing revealed she was 25% Jewish. Her staunchly Catholic Mexican family exploded: "The test is wrong." "We're pure Spanish blood." "How dare you suggest..."

But her great-aunt pulled her aside: "Your great-grandmother. During the war. She hid who she was to survive. We all knew but never spoke it."

Three generations of hidden identity. Three generations performing extra Catholicism to bury the truth. Three generations of children feeling the disconnection but never knowing why.

When Secrets Become Symptoms

What's mentionable is manageable. What's archived becomes symptomatic. Secrets don't stay contained in their folders. They leak into family life as behavioral symptoms—compulsive repetition of hidden patterns, phobias linked to secret events, addiction cycling through generations. They manifest as emotional symptoms—unexplained anxiety or depression, grief for unknown losses, shame without source, fear without memory. They appear as physical symptoms—illness anniversaries, psychosomatic pain, fertility issues, chronic conditions.

Catalina's family demonstrated this perfectly. Three generations of women with "nervous stomachs" requiring medication. When Catalina finally unarchived the family secret—her great-grandmother's death from a botched abortion—the pattern clicked.

"Every woman in our family has stomach problems. We're literally gut-sick from a secret about women's bodies and choice. Our bodies remember what our mouths can't speak."

The ACE (Adverse Childhood Experiences) Study found that family secrets correlate with higher rates of autoimmune disease (+70%), depression (+300%), addiction (+400%), and early death (+20 years average) [RS]. Keeping secrets costs more than telling them, but the bill comes in ways we don't always recognize.

Digital Archaeology and The Unarchiving Process

Modern technology has become an unexpected archaeologist, excavating what families buried. Facebook suggests relatives you didn't know existed. DNA tests reveal ethnic backgrounds that contradict family lore. Tagged photos surface from events that "never happened."

Jason's family secret unraveled through Instagram. His cousin posted a throwback photo: "Miss you, Uncle Mike!" Jason had no Uncle Mike. Never heard of him. But there in the photo—his father's face, younger, standing next to a man who looked exactly like him.

The algorithm had surfaced what the family buried: his father's twin brother, exiled thirty years ago for being gay. Erased so completely that Jason's generation didn't know he existed.

"The internet remembered what we were forced to forget," Jason said. "One tag, and thirty years of erasure crumbled."

But secrets are like archaeological sites—excavate too fast, and you destroy what you're trying to preserve. Too slow, and another generation inherits the burial ground. The unarchiving process requires delicate balance.

Before opening archives, build a support system. Secure a therapy relationship. Prepare for family upheaval. Consider everyone affected. Plan for various reactions. Sandy started with gentle questions: Why did Grandma hate hospitals? What happened to the baby clothes in the attic? Why don't we have photos from 1975-1978? Who was the woman in the torn photo? Each question a key to a locked file.

Learning the secret is step one. Integrating it—making meaning, finding healing, rewriting the family story—that's the real work. Not every secret needs unarchiving. Some truths serve no one. Ask yourself: Will revealing help healing? Who bears the cost of truth? Is this my secret to tell? What's the motivation for revealing? Can relationships survive the truth?

Margaret chose selective unarchiving. Her mother's affair? Revealed, because it explained the divorce. Her father's war crimes? Remained archived, because he'd faced justice and showing her children would only traumatize.

"Some secrets are like toxic waste," she explained. "You can't just dump them anywhere. They need proper containment, proper handling, or they poison everything they touch."

Your Seven-Day Secret Assessment Challenge

Week 8 of your 90-day transformation—focuses on **Examining** family secrets' impact.

Daily Focus:

Day	Activity
Monday	Notice one topic your family avoids
Tuesday	Ask one gentle question about family history
Wednesday	Journal about sensed-but-unspoken truths
Thursday	Research one family inconsistency
Friday	Share one truth about yourself
Saturday	Practice sitting with uncomfortable revelations
Sunday	Honor both truth and timing

One Key Question to Carry This Week: *"What family truth am I sensing but not speaking?"*

The Power of Examination (Round Two)

Now you're examining at archaeological depth:

- Understanding how secrets shape family dynamics
- Seeing connections between symptoms and hidden truths
- Recognizing which secrets need revealing vs. containing
- Examining impact across generations

Remember: You don't have to unarchive everything. Some secrets are best transformed through healing their effects.

Recovery Log: Nathan, Year 2

Found out more about Thomas, the brother I never knew existed. Mom finally opened up—he wasn't just sick, he had a heart defect they couldn't fix in 1979. She kept every hospital bracelet, every photo, even the blanket he was wrapped in. Explained everything—why she panicked when any of us got sick. Why she hovered at every playground. Why May 15th was always "migraine day." The secret shaped us all. My anxiety about my own kids' health, Sister's decision not to have children, Mom's obsession with medical checkups. Now we know. Now we can grieve properly.

The archive is open, and we're all finally breathing..

Next: Chapter 9 explores how families limit healing to "approved" methods—and why breaking free to explore new modalities might be the key to transformation.

… … … // buffering … … …

<CHAPTER_9>
THE EXPLORE PAGE OF HEALING //

Discovering new modalities...

74% complete

Remember Pokémon Go? Millions suddenly explored neighborhoods they'd ignored for years, finding treasures in familiar places. Healing works the same way—the solutions exist all around you, but your family's algorithm keeps you walking the same routes, blind to alternatives.

Veronica sat in my office after three years of traditional talk therapy, frustrated to the point of tears. "I can explain exactly why I'm anxious," she said. "I have PowerPoints about my trauma. I understand my mother's criticism stems from her mother's criticism. I can trace the pattern back four generations. But knowing why doesn't stop the panic attacks."

Her family believed in thinking your way out of problems. Books were medicine. Analysis was healing. They'd mock anything that seemed "woo-woo"—meditation was for people who couldn't think properly, medication was weakness, body work was new-age nonsense.

But her panic attacks didn't care about her analysis. They lived in her body, not her mind. And her family's approved healing method—thinking harder—was like trying to put out a fire with gasoline.

The Family Filter Bubble: Your Limited Healing Menu

Only 23% of people seek healing modalities outside their family's comfort zone [CS]. The other 77% try to solve problems using the same tools that created them. Your algorithm literally prevents you from discovering solutions by hiding them from your explore page.

From a postmodern perspective, families create "healing hierarchies"—stories about which ways of seeking help are acceptable. These narratives are passed down unconsciously, limiting each generation to the same approaches.

Every family has its preferred healing stories:

The Intellectualizers: Understanding equals healing, but embodied knowing is dismissed

The Spiritualizers: Faith fixes everything, but professional help means failed faith

The Medicalizers: Only doctors have answers, but holistic approaches are quackery

The Bootstrappers: Strength solves all, but vulnerability equals weakness

Jennifer's family were Bootstrappers. When panic attacks started, the family algorithm activated: "You're stronger than this." "Our family doesn't do therapy." It took her sister's suicide attempt for the family narrative to crack enough to allow different stories.

Your family gave you one recipe for healing. The world offers a thousand. The healing landscape has expanded exponentially, offering multiple ways of knowing and transforming. Traditional approaches include Cognitive-Behavioral Therapy (CBT) for thought patterns, psychodynamic therapy for unconscious processes, family systems for relational dynamics. Postmodern approaches like narrative therapy help you re-author your life story—anxiety becomes "the anxiety" that visits you, not who you are. Internal Family Systems (IFS) helps you dialogue with different aspects of yourself—not as pathology, but as natural multiplicity we all possess.

Somatic approaches honor the body's wisdom through EMDR (Eye Movement Desensitization and Reprocessing), Somatic Experiencing, breathwork. Skill-based approaches like DBT (Dialectical Behavior Therapy) offer concrete tools for overwhelming emotions. Creative therapies use art, music, drama to access wisdom beyond language.

The Revolutionary Discovery of Parts

Aaron had been in therapy for years when I suggested IFS "You want me to talk to parts of myself? Like I have multiple personalities?" he asked skeptically.

"Not multiple personalities," I explained. "From an IFS perspective, multiplicity is normal. We all have different parts—the angry teenager who protected you, the perfectionist who earned love, the scared child who needs comfort. None are pathological—they're all trying to help."

In his first IFS session, Aaron met his "protector"—a teenage version of himself, arms crossed, radiating anger. "I've been keeping us safe since Dad started raging," the part told him. "You needed me then. But I'm exhausted from being on guard for thirty years."

For the first time, Aaron felt curious about his anger instead of ashamed. He wasn't broken—he had parts still protecting him from dangers that had passed.

"It changed my whole story," Aaron said. "Instead of 'I have an anger problem,' it became 'I have a protective part that needs to know we're safe now.'"

When Different Works: Breaking Through Resistance

Different modalities offer different ways of knowing and healing. Jennifer discovered this when she reluctantly tried DBT skills group. "I want to understand my story, not memorize acronyms," she protested.

But DBT offered tools her family never imagined. When panic visited, she learned TIPP: Temperature change (cold water on face), Intense exercise (twenty jumping jacks), Paced breathing (out longer than in), Paired muscle relaxation.

"My family's only crisis skill was 'suck it up,'" Jennifer reflected. "DBT gave me actual tools. When panic visits, I can change my body temperature instead of white-knuckling through."

When you explore forbidden modalities, expect internal resistance. Rosa's Mexican Catholic family had strong stories about healing: problems stay in family, prayer provides answers, therapy means failed faith.

When Rosa started therapy, guilt became loud. But exploring this from an IFS lens, asking her to get curious about her "guilty part," something shifted.

"I realized Guilt wasn't me—it was a part trying to keep me connected to my family. Once I could appreciate its protective intention while choosing differently, everything changed."

Creating Your Healing Portfolio: The Collaborative Approach

From a collaborative therapy stance, you're the expert on what combination serves your unique story. Healing isn't about finding THE way—it's about discovering what helps you access more choices.

Maya's healing portfolio evolved over five years. Year 1: Narrative therapy to re-author her story. Year 2: Added IFS to befriend her internal community. Year 3: Incorporated DBT skills and EMDR. Year 4: Added yoga and meditation. Year 5: Flexible combination based on current needs.

"IFS helped me understand I have parts, like everyone. Narrative therapy helped me see anxiety as something that visits, not who I am. DBT gave me tools. Each approach offered different gifts."

The magic isn't in choosing one perfect modality—it's in becoming curious about what combination supports your unique system. Like a DJ mixing tracks, you can blend approaches to create your personal healing soundtrack.

Your Seven-Day Healing Exploration Challenge

Week 9 of your 90-day transformation—you're **Challenging** your family's healing limitations.

Daily Focus:

Day	Activity
Monday	List your family's approved/forbidden healing methods
Tuesday	Research one modality you've never considered
Wednesday	Talk to someone who healed differently than expected
Thursday	Try one 10-minute new practice
Friday	Notice resistance as protective story, not truth
Saturday	Book one new healing experience
Sunday	Celebrate exploring beyond comfort zone

One Key Question to Carry This Week: *"What story is the part of me that fears new healing methods trying to tell?"*

The Power of Challenge (Round Two)

Now you're challenging at the level of possibility:

- Questioning inherited healing hierarchies
- Testing if forbidden approaches might help
- Challenging the idea that one way works for all
- Opening to multiple ways of knowing

Remember: You don't need to adopt everything. You're expanding options, not replacing all current supports.

Recovery Log: Maya, Day 459

Family thought I'd lost my story. Therapy AND IFS AND DBT skills AND medication? "Pick one!" they said. But my experience needed different approaches for different chapters. IFS helped me befriend my anxious part. DBT gave me actual tools. Narrative therapy helped me see anxiety as a visitor, not identity. Today marks one year panic-free. Turns out I didn't need to think harder—I needed more stories about who I could be.

Next: Chapter 10 reveals how to update your emotional programming—not just for yourself, but to co-author new possibilities for future generations.

… … … // buffering … … …

<CHAPTER_10>
ALGORITHM UPDATE //

Installing new responses...

82% complete

The Ten-Year Challenge showed our physical transformations but imagine posting your emotional evolution: 2014 You are running toxic patterns vs 2024 You are modeling healthy boundaries. That's the glow-up that actually matters—updating your internal algorithm for generational change.

The notification appeared on Kenji's therapy homework app: "Update Available: Install Emotional Security Patch 2.0?"

After two years of collaborative work, Kenji was ready to co-author a new story, to choose different responses than his father's programming dictated.

His old story: When conflict appears, I disappear. Emotions are dangerous. Resolution is impossible. I repeat my father's patterns.

His emerging story: When conflict appears, I can breathe first. Emotions are information. Resolution is possible through presence. I can co-create new patterns with my family.

The update wasn't just for him. Kenji's seven-year-old son watched everything, downloading his father's responses as possibility. Every healthy reaction Kenji modeled was a new chapter in his son's developing story.

The Science of Rewiring

Neuroplasticity research shows the human brain can form new neural pathways at any age, with the most dramatic rewiring possible between ages 25-45 [RS]. You're not stuck with your inherited code—you're in the prime window for comprehensive updates.

Dr. Rick Hanson's research proves "neurons that fire together, wire together" [RS]. Each time you choose a new response over an old pattern, you literally rebuild your brain architecture. It takes approximately 66 repetitions to establish a new neural pathway [RS].

The brain doesn't care about your insights—it cares about your repetitions. Understanding why you're anxious is one form of knowledge. Repeatedly choosing calm responses creates embodied knowing.

Priya's 90-day experiment showed how change happens through practice, not just understanding. During the first month, she simply noticed anxiety patterns—about 47 times daily [CS]. No judgment, just witnessing. "I'm becoming a curious observer of my own story," she said.

The second month brought active experimentation. She caught pattern activation (now down to 35 times daily) and tried one different response each time. Small edits to her story. Tiny rebellions against inherited plot lines. Some worked, some didn't, but each attempt built new neural pathways.

By the third month, new responses felt more natural than old patterns. Anxiety episodes dropped 70% [CS]. "Day 67 was magic," Priya recalled. "My mother criticized my parenting—the usual activation. But instead of defending or collapsing, I just said, 'Thanks for sharing your perspective.' My body stayed calm. My daughter watched me not crumble. Three generations of women, and the story finally changed."

The key was repetition, not perfection. Each time Priya chose differently, she strengthened the new neural pathway. Like water carving a new channel through rock, consistency created permanent change.

Implementing Change Across Generations

Like any software update, new patterns need testing in safe environments before full implementation. But unlike personal updates, generational change requires conscious modeling for those who come after.

Kevin created what he called his "boundary practice lab." He started with the lowest stakes possible—saying no to phone solicitors, setting limits with chatty neighbors. "I'm building my 'no' muscle," he explained. These interactions mattered because they were practice runs with no real consequences.

He then progressed to medium stakes with work colleagues and casual friends. Each successful boundary-built confidence for the next. By the time he faced his family gatherings—what he called "boss level"—he had over 100 practice runs. "Still challenging, but I had new muscle memory. My body knew how to stay calm while setting limits."

The real transformation came when Kevin realized his changes were rippling outward. The Williams family anger story had been passed down for four generations. Great-grandfather's war trauma wrote the first chapter—rage as survival. Grandfather's chapter added alcohol to numb the rage. Father's chapter included holes punched in walls, thrown objects, family fear.

Robert became meticulous about re-authoring this narrative. He mapped his anger's visiting patterns, noticing it arrived most often when he felt powerless. He created a "circuit breaker" protocol—physical movement to discharge the energy. He developed repair practices for any slips. Most importantly, he began modeling alternatives in real-time.

"I realized I was ghost-writing my son's future story," Robert told me. "Every time I exploded, I was teaching him that men handle feelings through destruction."

"My son saw me furious yesterday," Robert shared. "Really furious. The old me would have hidden it or exploded. But he saw me say, 'I need a minute,' walk outside, do jumping jacks, come back calm. He witnessed anger visiting without destruction following. That's four generations of storytelling, finally evolving."

The change wasn't just behavioral—it was neurological. Robert's son's brain was forming different neural pathways than Robert's had. Where Robert learned "anger equals destruction," his son was learning "anger equals information requiring skillful response." The family algorithm was updating in real-time.

Navigating Family Resistance to Change

When you update your algorithm, the family system often panics. You're not just changing personal habits—you're disrupting a multi-generational narrative. The resistance can be fierce because your healing threatens the entire system's homeostasis.

Linda discovered this when her family staged an intervention. Her crimes? Setting boundaries, expressing needs, declining the role of family emotional caretaker. They gathered in her mother's living room to explain how her "selfishness" was "destroying the family."

"The old me would have crumbled," Linda reflected. "Apologized, resumed my role, buried my needs again. But I'd been practicing my new story for months. I took a deep breath and said, 'I love you all, and I'm going to keep choosing health. You're welcome to join me in writing new chapters.'"

The room erupted. Her father stormed out. Her mother cried. Two siblings followed Dad. But something remarkable happened. Her younger sister stayed. Her brother asked quietly, "What chapters are you writing?" Her cousin texted later: "Can we talk?"

This is how system change happens—not through confrontation but through consistent modeling. You can't force updates on anyone's system. You can only live such a compelling new story that others become curious about co-authoring their own changes.

Brandon discovered this truth after becoming his family's first therapy success story. He never preached or pushed. He simply became what he called the family's "soft place to land." As relatives noticed his transformation—less anger, more presence, actual boundaries—they began approaching him privately.

His brother wondered about therapy options. His sister asked about meditation apps. His mother, after two years of watching, finally whispered at a family dinner, "How did you stop being so angry? I want to learn."

"I never tried to convert anyone," Brandon explained. "I just lived a different story consistently. They couldn't unsee the possibility. When they were ready, they asked."

Research confirms this ripple effect. When one family member does deep healing work, 73% report at least one family member seeking help within two years [AS]. Nearly half see positive changes in family dynamics without others doing formal work. Your update creates ripples because stories are contagious. Even family members who initially resist are affected. They can't unhear the new narrative, can't unfeel the possibility, can't return to complete unconsciousness about the old story's limitations.

Your Seven-Day Update Installation Challenge

Week 10 of your 90-day transformation—you're practicing **Override** at mastery level.

Daily Focus:

Day	Activity
Monday	Choose one pattern to update
Tuesday	Design your new response
Wednesday	Practice in low-stakes situation
Thursday	Implement with medium challenge
Friday	Notice resistance as the old story protesting
Saturday	Celebrate any new response
Sunday	Plan next week's practice

One Key Question to Carry This Week: *"What story am I ready to stop inheriting and start rewriting?"*

The Power of Override (Round Two)

Now you're overriding at the level of legacy:

- Not just changing personal responses but family narratives
- Creating new possibilities for future generations
- Overriding multi-generational patterns
- Installing updates that will outlive you

Remember: Every healthy choice rewrites code that's run for generations.

Recovery Log: Robert, Day 729

Two years since I started updating my story. Today my teenage son said, "Dad, I notice when I'm getting triggered now. Like you showed me—breathe first, respond second." I cried. Forty years of men in my family rage-reacting, and he's already authoring a different story at 14. The update worked. The narrative is changing. The future holds new possibilities.

Next: Chapter 11 examines how families curate their public image while struggling privately—and why closing the gap between performance and authenticity transforms everything.

... ... // buffering ... ...

<CHAPTER_11>
THE HIGHLIGHT REEL VS. REALITY //

Comparing public/private feeds...

90% complete

Remember the Instagram vs. Reality trend? Split screens showing the perfect photo next to the chaotic truth. Your family has been running this split screen for generations—curated perfection hiding dysfunction. Time to close the gap between performance and truth.

The Mitchell's looked flawless on Facebook. Coordinated Christmas cards, vacation highlights, achievement announcements. Lauren Mitchell's feed was #FamilyGoals incarnate.

Behind the algorithm: Dad's hidden gambling debt of $147,000. Mom's wine bottle graveyard in the garage. Perfect son's third stint in rehab. Honor student daughter's cutting scars. Family therapy sessions every Thursday.

"We spent more time staging photos than actually connecting," Lauren confessed. "I'd scream at everyone to smile, threaten consequences for ruining the shot, then post about our 'blessed life.' The performance was killing us."

Their Thanksgiving post—47 likes, 12 heart emojis, "Beautiful family!" comments—was taken between Dad storming out and Mom's breakdown. The tablecloth hid wine stains. The smiles lasted exactly 3.7 seconds.

91% of families curate their public image while privately struggling [IS]. The average family spends four times more energy maintaining their facade than addressing their actual experiences [CS]. Your exhaustion isn't from your challenges—it's from pretending they don't exist.

The Hidden Cost of Performance

From a narrative therapy perspective, families often get trapped between their "preferred story" (what they show the world) and their "lived story" (what actually happens). The gap between these narratives creates immense suffering that compounds across generations.

Every family has performance metrics—what they measure and display versus what actually matters. Traditional family dashboards showcase external achievement, public reputation, social media engagement, material success. Never measured: emotional safety, authentic connection, mental wellbeing, individual growth, genuine joy.

The Kim family ran entirely on achievement metrics. Their refrigerator showcased college acceptance letters, medical school graduations. Never displayed: therapy appointment cards, antidepressant prescriptions, suicide attempt discharge papers, divorce lawyer business cards."We were winning at everything that didn't matter," daughter Grace realized. "Losing at everything that did."

Harvard's Grant Study followed families for 75 years, finding those who prioritized image over authenticity had three times higher addiction rates, five times more anxiety disorders, double the divorce probability, and 70% less life satisfaction [RS]. The performance itself became the pathology.

The toxic comparison loop makes it worse. You see other families' highlights, feel inadequate, increase performance pressure, post your own highlights, perpetuate the cycle. Social media didn't invent family comparison—it just digitized it, making the highlight reels inescapable.

Holly watched her sister-in-law's Instagram stories obsessively. Perfect house, perfect children, perfect marriage. It made Holly's beautifully ordinary life feel like failure. Until the perfect sister-in-law called at 2 AM, sobbing. The perfect husband had been cheating for years. The perfect children were in therapy. The perfect house was in foreclosure.

"But your Instagram..." Holly said, stunned.

"Is a lie," her sister-in-law whispered. "I post the life I wish I had."

The Patel family calculated their "perfection invoice"—what maintaining the facade actually cost. Financially: private school they couldn't afford ($40K/year), luxury car leases for image ($1,500/month), country club membership ($15K/year), designer clothes for events ($20K/year). Emotionally: Mom's anxiety medication, Dad's 60-hour work weeks, son's eating disorder, daughter's complete disconnection, family intimacy nonexistent.

"We were broke financially and emotionally," Mom admitted. "Spending everything we didn't have to impress people who didn't care about our real story."

Breaking Free from the Performance

The revolution begins with one family member saying: "I can't do this anymore." One person stepping out of performance into truth, refusing to maintain the exhausting charade.

Michael started his family's uprising at Easter dinner. The table was set perfectly, the food Instagram-worthy, everyone dressed in their Sunday best. His hands shook as he pushed back from the table.

"I need to tell you all something. I'm... I'm seeing a therapist. For depression. And Janet and I are having problems."

His mother's fork clattered to her plate. "Michael, this isn't the time—"

"When is the time, Mom? When do we ever talk about anything real?"

An uncomfortable silence stretched. His father cleared his throat and changed the subject to the game. His sister scrolled through her phone. His teenage niece watched with wide eyes but said nothing.

The dinner continued with strained small talk. But later, as Michael helped clear dishes, his brother followed him to the kitchen. "Hey, about what you said... I've been thinking about therapy too. Can you send me your person's info?"

It wasn't a revolution. It was a crack in the facade. Three months later, his niece texted him: "Uncle Mike, can we talk? I'm struggling with some stuff." Small shifts, not seismic ones. The family photos still looked perfect, but now a few of them knew the truth behind the smiles.

Breaking the highlight reel addiction rarely happens through organized family meetings and structured changes. The Johnson family's wake-up call came when their son had an anxiety attack while staging another "perfect" Christmas photo. As his mother demanded "real smiles this time," the 12-year-old started hyperventilating, tears streaming down his face.

"Just take the damn picture without me!" he screamed, running to his room.

The remaining family members stood frozen in their coordinated outfits. They took the photo anyway - minus one family member. Mom posted it with some excuse about their son being sick.

That night, Dad found his wife crying while scrolling through other families' Christmas posts. "Maybe we should... ease up on the photos," he suggested tentatively. She nodded but didn't delete the post.

Change came in fits and starts. Mom tried to stage fewer photos, but old habits die hard. During spring break, she caught herself arranging everyone for the perfect beach shot until her daughter said, "Mom, can we just swim?"

They didn't institute formal guidelines or have family meetings. Instead, small shifts accumulated: Dad started leaving his phone in the car during dinners - sometimes. The kids began opting out of photos - mom protested but eventually accepted it. Their son's therapist suggested limiting social media, which helped his anxiety, though Mom still struggled with the urge to document everything.

"I used to get hundreds of likes," Mom admitted to a friend six months later, showing a candid photo with only 47 hearts. "Part of me misses it. I know that's shallow, but... it made me feel like I was doing something right as a mother."

The family's transformation was messy and incomplete. Mom still occasionally pushed for staged photos. Their Instagram feed became a mix - some performed moments when Mom insisted, some genuine candid's when Dad took the phone. Their son's anxiety improved somewhat, though family photos remained a trigger. Their daughter learned to firmly say "no" to photos she didn't want taken.

Two years later, they were still finding their balance between sharing and performing, privacy and connection. Not a revolution - just a slow, imperfect evolution toward something more real.

Creating Authentic Connection

When families drop their facades, research shows remarkable impacts. 67% report closer relationships within six months [AS]. Anxiety decreases significantly. Others begin sharing more authentically. Nearly all wish they'd done it sooner.

Your authenticity gives others permission to drop their performance. When you stop pretending, you create space for real connection. The goal isn't swinging from false perfection to performative messiness. It's finding integration—sharing authentically while maintaining healthy privacy.

The Martinez family reunion transformed slowly after Grandma planted a seed at her 80th birthday. During the typical rounds of glossy speeches about their wonderful family, she simply said:

"You know, Rodrigo and I had rough patches. Really rough. I hope you all know it's okay if your marriages aren't perfect either."

The room went quiet. Someone nervously laughed. Someone else quickly raised a toast to change the subject. The moment passed.

But Grandma had opened a door. Over the next hour, her daughter pulled her aside: "Mom, what you said... thank you. Tom and I are actually in counseling."

At the next family gathering six months later, that daughter mentioned their therapy casually, testing the waters. A cousin admitted she was on antidepressants. An uncle mentioned his AA meetings—something everyone knew but never discussed.

It took three years before the family culture genuinely shifted. Not everyone participated. Some relatives still insisted on the performance. But pockets of authenticity formed—cousins who texted real support, siblings who could discuss struggles, a grandmother who kept gently modeling that imperfection was acceptable.

The reunion photos still looked polished. But now, some family members also had a group chat called "The Real Real" where they shared what was actually happening in their lives. Progress, not perfection.

Your Seven-Day Reality Check Challenge

Week 11 of your 90-day transformation—focuses on **Downloading** authentic ways of being.

Daily Focus:

Day	Action
Monday	Notice one family performance you maintain
Tuesday	Share one imperfection with someone safe
Wednesday	Post (or don't post) authentically
Thursday	Celebrate an ordinary, unposed moment

Day	Action
Friday	Admit one struggle to family
Saturday	Connect without documenting
Sunday	Appreciate unperformed reality

One Key Question to Carry This Week: *"What would happen if we valued connection over impression?"*

The Power of Download (Round Two)

Now you're downloading at the level of family culture:

- Integrating authenticity as new family norm
- Repeatedly choosing connection over performance
- Building evidence that real is better than perfect
- Creating new family stories based on truth

Remember: You're not just dropping your mask—you're changing what masks mean in your family system.

Recovery Log: Lauren, Day 912

Three years ago, our Christmas card was a lie—coordinated outfits hiding crisis. This year? We sent a photo of us in therapy together. The card said, "Working on our stories, grateful for growth." Lost some Facebook friends. Gained actual family connection. My kids now know love doesn't require perfection. It requires presence. The facade is down. We're free.

Next: Chapter 12 explores how one person's healing journey can spread through families and communities—becoming patient zero for generational health rather than generational trauma.

… … … // buffering … … …

<CHAPTER_12>
GOING VIRAL FOR GOOD //

Spreading healing.exe...

98% complete

Remember the Ice Bucket Challenge? 17 million people dumped ice water on themselves, raising $115 million for ALS research. Healing can spread the same way—one person's visible transformation inspiring countless others to begin their journey. You're about to become patient zero for generational health.

Marcus traced his healing ripples like a sociologist mapping viral spread. It started with him—panic attacks driving him to therapy. Within two months, his wife joined couples therapy. By month four, his brother asked for a therapist referral. Month six, his best friend started meditation.

The second ring spread further. His wife's sister left a toxic relationship. His brother's wife started antidepressants. His friend's partner began anger management. By year two, his nephew felt comfortable expressing emotions. His niece sought help for anxiety. His friend's kids were growing up with therapy normalized.

"I just wanted to stop having panic attacks," Marcus marveled. "I had no idea I was starting an epidemic of healing."

One person's healing journey impacts an average of 127 people across three generations [AS]. Like a viral video, healing spreads exponentially—but unlike toxic content, its effects compound positively over time.

The Science and Art of Healing Contagion

MIT research on social contagion shows that behaviors spread through networks with predictable patterns. Healing behaviors are three times more contagious than toxic ones when modeled consistently [RS]. Your transformation is literally infectious—in the best way.

Dr. Nicholas Christakis's groundbreaking studies found that your behavior influences your friends by 45%, your friends' friends by 25%, and even your friends' friends' friends by 15% [RS]. Effects remain visible up to three degrees of separation. You don't need millions of followers to create change. Real influence happens in intimate networks, through authentic connection, via consistent modeling.

Sarah never posted about therapy on social media. Never made grand announcements. But people noticed her transformation—her calm during family chaos, her boundaries with difficult people, her expanding emotional vocabulary, her improving marriage, her visibly decreasing anxiety.

"How?" they started asking. One by one. Privately. Quietly.

Sarah became what I call a "healing dealer"—distributing tools, resources, and hope to anyone ready. Her phone became a repository of resources: twelve people she'd referred to therapy, eight who'd joined her meditation group, fifteen who'd borrowed her books, six who called during crisis moments, three siblings transforming their parenting.

"I'm not trying to convert anyone," sheexplained. "I just live my healing out loud, and people ask for the recipe."

The key to Natalie's influence wasn't preaching—it was consistency. She didn't just talk about boundaries; she lived them. She didn't lecture about self-care; she modeled it. When family members tested her new patterns, she held steady. When work demanded old behaviors, she maintained her changes. This consistency created trust. People saw the changes weren't temporary or performative—they were real, sustainable transformation.

Breaking the Chain of Trauma Transmission

From a narrative therapy perspective, trauma travels through families like an unwanted heirloom until someone is brave enough to transform it into wisdom. The opposite of viral healing is viral trauma—pain spreading unconsciously through generations. But here's the revolutionary truth: healing is more contagious than trauma when it's made visible.

The Johnson family trauma had spread for four generations like a multigenerational virus. Grandfather's war trauma manifested as rage and alcoholism. This infected his son with childhood abuse leading to emotional absence. The third generation inherited emotional neglect resulting in anxiety and control. By the fourth generation, anxious parenting was creating... what?

Maria (Generation 3) decided the transmission stopped with her. She started with what seemed like a simple conversation at dinner.

"I want to talk about how I've been as a mom," she began. Her teenagers immediately tensed.

"Is this about my grades?" her son asked.

"Are you dying?" her daughter added.

"No, I—I've been in therapy. Learning about our family patterns." Maria's rehearsed speech crumbled. "I was too controlling. Because my parents... because I was anxious..."

"Mom, you're being weird," her daughter said, returning to her phone.

Her son just shrugged. "Can I go?"

The conversation died. Maria's grand moment of breaking generational patterns had lasted under three minutes.

She tried again two weeks later. This time her daughter rolled her eyes. "Mom, we get it. You're in therapy. Good for you."

But she kept going—messily, imperfectly. Apologizing at random moments. "Sorry I freaked out about your room. That's my anxiety, not your problem." Getting blank stares. Trying again anyway.

Six months in, her son mentioned casually, "Mom's been different. Less... hovery."

"Still annoying though," her daughter added. But later, privately, she asked Maria for her therapist's number. "Not because I need it. Just curious."

A year later, mid-argument about curfew, her daughter suddenly said, "Wait, are you being controlling because of Grandpa's PTSD thing?"

Progress. Messy, non-linear, teenager-filtered progress.

Maria still slips. Last month she monitored her son's whereabouts obsessively, then caught herself. "Sorry. I'm doing the thing again."

"Yeah, you are," he said. But he hugged her after.

The virus of trauma met the imperfect antidote of trying. Some days it works. Some days it doesn't. The transmission is weakening, not in a straight line but in spirals and loops and teenage eye rolls.

Creating Healing Networks and Content

Healing spreads fastest through vulnerable shares, not perfect presentations. People don't need your success story—they need your struggle story with hope attached. The vulnerability itself becomes medicine.

Michael learned this at his company town hall. Asked about work-life balance, instead of corporate platitudes, he shared truth: "Honestly? I'm in therapy because I realized I'm repeating my dad's workaholism. I missed my daughter's recital last month and saw my father's ghost in the mirror. I'm working on presence over productivity. It's hard. I'm learning."

The room shifted. Energy changed. Executives became humans. Within six months, the company culture transformed: mental health days implemented, emotional intelligence added to leadership training, therapy coverage expanded, 40% of staff sought mental health support [CS].

"I thought vulnerability would end my career," Andy reflected. "Instead, it transformed our entire corporate culture. My openness gave 400 people permission to prioritize their mental health."

In the digital age, your healing can literally go viral through intentional sharing. The Martinez family created their own #HeritageHealing challenge, documenting their journey from addiction and abuse patterns to connected relationships and emotional safety. They created a private Facebook group that became a healing archive: old patterns identified, therapy wins celebrated, setbacks normalized, resources shared, progress tracked, hope maintained.

"My kids will never wonder if change is possible," Mom declared. "They have 500 posts proving it is."

Lisa took a different approach with public healing content. Instead of highlight reels, she shared therapy parking lot selfies with captions about what she was working on. She posted meditation timer screenshots showing her daily practice. She shared book recommendations with personal notes about what helped. Her follower count stayed modest (847), but her impact went deep—73 DMs from people starting therapy, 45 friends trying meditation, 12 people leaving toxic relationships.

"I'm not an influencer," Lisa laughed. "I'm more like healing middleware—connecting people to resources they didn't know existed."

The key to creating healing content is authenticity without overexposure. Share your journey, not your entire therapy session. Offer hope, not false promises. Provide resources, not prescriptions. Model boundaries even in your sharing.

Building Sustainable Healing Communities

Unlike trauma that depletes over generations, healing appreciates in value. The compound interest is remarkable. Year 1 brings personal symptom reduction. Year 5 shows family system transformation. Year 10 reveals generational patterns broken. By Year 20, grandchildren are born into health, healing is normalized, and the trauma cycle is ancient history.

David calculated his healing ROI after a decade. Investment: Therapy. Returns: marriage saved ($50K divorce avoided), kids thriving (no therapy needed yet), career advanced through emotional intelligence, health improved (no stress-related illness), parents seeking help, siblings transforming. "Best investment I ever made," he concluded. "The returns keep multiplying."

You don't need a platform to spread healing. You need consistency, vulnerability, and strategic sharing. Think of it as concentric circles of influence. Your inner circle gets full transparency—immediate family sees everything age-appropriately. The middle circle receives selective sharing—extended family, close friends see strategic vulnerability. The outer circle experiences your boundaries authenticity—social media, professional spaces, strangers see appropriate glimpses.

Not everyone wants healing to spread. Dysfunctional systems resist change. Elana's family tried to quarantine her healing, mocking therapy, dismissing progress, excluding her from events. "They treated my healing like a virus to contain," Elena observed. "Which proved how threatening health was to their sickness."

She kept healing anyway. Slowly, the resisters became curious. The mockers became seekers. The virus they tried to stop had already spread. By year three, even the strongest opponents were asking for resources—privately, quietly, but asking, nonetheless.

Your Seven-Day Viral Healing Challenge

Week 12 of your 90-day transformation—focuses on **Evolving** into a healing catalyst.

Daily Focus:

Day	Action
Monday	Share one healing win with someone
Tuesday	Offer one resource to a seeker
Wednesday	Post authentically about growth
Thursday	Thank someone who inspired your healing
Friday	Make your progress visible to family
Saturday	Connect two people who could help each other
Sunday	Celebrate the ripples you've created

One Key Question to Carry This Week: *"How can my healing give others permission to write their own story?"*

The Power of Evolve (Final Stage)

You've reached the pinnacle of DECODE—evolution. Now you're:

- Transforming from healed to healer
- Creating ripples that outlive you
- Building healing infrastructure for others
- Evolving your entire family system

Remember: Your healing isn't just personal—it's generational medicine.

Recovery Log: Marcus, Day 1,095

Three years ago, I started therapy to save myself. Today, my entire family is in healing. My kids will never know the generational trauma that shaped us for centuries. They're growing up with emotional intelligence, boundaries, and the radical idea that asking for help is strength. The trauma stopped with me. The healing started with me. And it spread like wildfire. We're not perfect—we're free.

Next: The Conclusion brings us full circle, revealing how rewriting your emotional algorithm transforms not just your life, but creates a living legacy that ripples through time.

… … … // buffering … … …

<CONCLUSION>

LEGACY CODE // Transformation complete. Saving changes...

Three years after that 2:47 AM notification, Sarah stood in her childhood bedroom, packing up her mother's things. Mom had died peacefully, her own healing journey just beginning when time ran out. She found the photo albums—the public one, pristine and performed, and the private one, full of candid chaos and actual joy.

She'd spent three years rewriting her emotional algorithm. Her old code insisted on hiding pain, performing perfection, silencing truth. Her new story embraced feeling fully, living authentically, speaking honestly.

But standing there, holding both albums, she realized something profound: She didn't have to choose. Both were true. Her family was performative AND loving. Dysfunctional AND devoted. Broken AND beautiful.

The algorithm had insisted on binary processing—good OR bad, healthy OR toxic, keep OR delete. But human hearts hold paradox. We can love people who hurt us. Honor parents who failed us. Grieve relationships that needed to end. Hold multiple truths without system crash.

"Mom," whispering to the empty room, "I debugged our code. Your grandchildren will know joy without performance. They'll feel without fear. The patterns stop here. The healing starts now. This is your legacy too—you gave me something to transform."

Your Transformation Journey

If you've made it this far, you've already begun the update. You've seen your patterns, questioned your programming, felt the possibility of change. The algorithm no longer runs invisibly—you've made it conscious. And consciousness is where choice lives.

Some of you have already set your first boundary, spoken your first truth, felt your first unmuted emotion, made your first different choice, inspired your first follower. Others are still gathering courage, still in the preparation phase, still deciding if change is possible. That's okay. Awakening happens in its own time. But know this: every moment you spend conscious of your patterns is a moment stolen from their power.

Children who witness their parents' healing journey are 400% more likely to seek help when needed, 300% better at emotional regulation, and 500% more likely to break their own inherited patterns [AS]. Your healing today becomes their emotional inheritance tomorrow.

Your children—biological, chosen, or spiritual—are watching. Not your performance, but your practice. Not your perfection, but your progress. They're downloading how you handle conflict, process pain, seek help, set boundaries, repair mistakes, choose growth. Every healthy response you model becomes available in their emotional dropdown menu. Every pattern you break removes a bug from their inherited code.

Alexandra's seven-year-old daughter demonstrated this last week. When frustrated with homework, instead of the family's traditional meltdown-to-criticism cycle, she said: "Mama, I'm getting frustrated. I need a pause to breathe like you do." She walked to the window, took five deep breaths, and returned calmer. "I'm ready to try again now."

Seven years old. Already running cleaner code than forty generations before her.

The Ripple Effect You've Created

The butterfly effect in family systems means that one person's healing journey can prevent three cases of depression in the next generation, two addiction cycles from repeating, five anxiety disorders from developing, four relationship patterns from replicating, and countless moments of unnecessary suffering [IS].

You'll never fully know your impact. The cousin who started therapy after watching your transformation. The neighbor who left an abusive relationship after hearing your boundary-setting. The coworker who got help for their drinking after your vulnerable share. The child who will grow up believing emotions are safe because they watched you feel.

Some ripples are visible—family members seeking help, relationships improving, patterns breaking. But most spread silently through the network of human connection, touching lives you'll never know about, preventing pain you'll never witness, creating possibilities you'll never see bloom.

Your family's emotional algorithm was written by people doing their best with limited tools, processing trauma with primitive code, surviving however they could. Honor that. They brought you this far. They gave you something to transform. Without their patterns, you'd have nothing to evolve beyond. Your pain has been your teacher, your trauma your catalyst, your inheritance your opportunity.

But you have tools they didn't. Knowledge they couldn't access. Support they never found. Possibilities they couldn't imagine. You get to be the update your lineage has been waiting for—not perfect, not complete, but conscious and choosing.

Your Living Legacy

Legacy isn't what you leave behind when you die. It's what you live out loud while you're here. *The Generational Algorithm* isn't just code—it's legacy. Every family has one, written in behaviors not bytes, transmitted through modeling not modems, inherited through connection not cables.

Your legacy is being written right now in how you spoke to yourself this morning, in the boundary you set yesterday, in the help you sought last month, in the pattern you broke last year, in the healing you're spreading today. Every interaction is code being written for future generations.

This book ends, but your download continues. Every day offers new opportunities to **Detect** inherited patterns, **Examine** their sources and costs, **Challenge** their necessity, **Override** with healthier choices, **Download** new ways of being, Evolve your family's future. The DECODE method isn't a one-time process—it's a way of living consciously in relationship with your patterns.

Some days you'll run old code—that's okay. Healing isn't linear. It's not about perfection; it's about progress. Not about never falling back; it's about falling forward. Not about fixing everything; it's about changing what you can. The goal was never to become someone without patterns—it was to become someone conscious of their patterns, able to choose rather than react, capable of updating rather than repeating.

As you close this book and open to your life, remember: You are not broken—you're running outdated software. You are not alone—millions are updating alongside you. You are not too late—neuroplasticity is lifelong. You are not too small—one person can shift generations. You are not stuck—change is always possible.

The work is hard. Some days it will feel impossible. You'll face resistance from family, from society, from your own programming. You'll have moments of wanting to reinstall the old algorithm because at least it was familiar. This is normal. This is the process. This is how generational change happens—one conscious choice at a time, one brave person at a time, one family system at a time.

Your Next Steps

The algorithm ends here. The human journey continues. The legacy transformation begins now.

Take the Emotional Algorithm Assessment (EAA) if you haven't already. Begin your 90-Day Transformation with Week 1 challenges. Most importantly, pass this book forward to someone ready to begin their own transformation.

Remember: You're not just reading a book. You're rewriting history. You're debugging the future. You're updating humanity, one family system at a time.

The notification that started Sarah's journey? She screenshot it. Saved it. Sometimes she looks at it and whispers "thank you." That moment of recognition, that crack in the code, that 2:47 AM awakening—it changed everything. Not just for her. For all of us. For generations she'll never meet but who will live freer because she chose to heal.

Your notification has appeared. Your moment of recognition is here. Your crack in the code is widening.

The algorithm is updated. The humans are free. The future is different.

Welcome to your transformation.

Final Recovery Log

Day 1,826. Five years since I discovered our family algorithm. Five years of debugging, updating, healing, spreading. My children don't know the weight I carried—they know the freedom I chose. My parents see the patterns now—it's never too late. My siblings are on their own journeys—the ripples continue.

Not just for me. For all of us. For generations I'll never meet but who will live freer because I chose to heal.

The algorithm is updated. The humans are free. The future is different.

—Sarah, grateful for the glitch that woke her up

UPDATE COMPLETE.

100%

> Generational patterns successfully rewritten

> System restart recommended

> Thank you for installing hope.exe

<APPENDIX_A>

EMOTIONAL ALGORITHM ASSESSMENT (E.A.A.) // Running diagnostic scan...

Introduction to the Assessment

The EAA is designed to help you identify patterns in your family's emotional programming. This isn't a diagnostic tool—it's a mirror to help you see the invisible code that's been running your emotional life.

Remember: There are no "good" or "bad" scores. Higher scores simply indicate more areas where updating your emotional algorithm might bring relief and freedom. Be honest with yourself as you respond. Your first instinct is usually the most accurate.

How to Take the Assessment

Find a quiet space where you won't be interrupted

Read each statement carefully

Rate your response from 1 (never) to 5 (always)

Go with your first instinct—don't overthink

Complete all questions in one sitting if possible

Calculate your score using the guide below

The Assessment

Rate each statement from 1 (never) to 5 (always):

Detection Phase: Recognizing Inherited Patterns

I notice myself repeating my parents' exact words or behaviors □

I feel physically tense around certain family members □

I struggle with the same issues my parents faced □

I hear my family's voice when I make decisions □

I react to situations the way my family would expect □

Pattern Recognition: Identifying Cycles

I attract partners similar to my difficult parent □

I handle conflict exactly like/opposite to my family □

I pass down rules I don't even believe in □

I feel guilty when breaking family traditions □

I recreate familiar dynamics even when they're painful □

System Glitches: Emotional Disruptions

My emotional reactions seem too big for the situation □

I shut down when certain topics arise ☐

I can't express certain emotions freely ☐

I feel trapped in relationship patterns ☐

My body reacts before my mind understands why ☐

Family Dynamics: Relational Patterns

I take responsibility for others' emotions ☐

I struggle to set boundaries with family ☐

I feel invisible or unheard in family settings ☐

I play a specific role that feels unchangeable ☐

Family gatherings leave me exhausted ☐

Generational Transmission: Passing It Down

I see my family patterns in my children ☐

I fear becoming like my parents ☐

I catch myself parenting from fear, not love ☐

I worry about what I'm modeling ☐

I see patterns repeating across generations ☐

Update Readiness: Capacity for Change

I'm willing to see my family patterns clearly ☐

I can imagine responding differently than my parents □

I believe change is possible for me □

I'm ready to be the one who breaks the cycle □

I have support for making changes □

Scoring Your Assessment

Add up all your responses: _____

Score Interpretation

30-60: Light Debugging Needed Your family algorithm has some minor bugs, but overall you've developed relatively healthy patterns. You might benefit from:

Fine-tuning specific responses

Addressing one or two sticky patterns

Preventive maintenance to avoid future issues

Continuing to model health for the next generation

61-90: Moderate System Updates Required Your emotional algorithm has several areas that could use updating. You're likely experiencing:

Regular conflicts between inherited patterns and desired responses

Some relationships affected by old programming

Physical or emotional symptoms from suppressed feelings

Awareness of patterns but difficulty changing them

91-120: Major Programming Overhaul Recommended Your inherited algorithm is significantly impacting your daily life. You might be experiencing:

Constant internal conflict between old patterns and new desires

Relationship difficulties stemming from family programming

Physical symptoms of emotional suppression

Strong awareness that change is needed but feeling stuck

121-150: Complete Algorithm Rewrite in Progress You're deeply aware of how family patterns are affecting every area of your life. This high score indicates:

Active consciousness of inherited patterns

Readiness for significant transformation

Possible crisis that's making change urgent

Strong motivation to break generational cycles

Understanding Your Subscores

Look at each section separately to identify specific areas for focus:

Detection Phase (Questions 1-5)

High scores (20-25): You're very aware of inherited patterns

Low scores (5-10): You might benefit from increased awareness

Pattern Recognition (Questions 6-10)

High scores (20-25): You clearly see repeating cycles

Low scores (5-10): Patterns might be unconscious

System Glitches (Questions 11-15)

High scores (20-25): Your body is signaling need for change

Low scores (5-10): You're relatively regulated

Family Dynamics (Questions 16-20)

High scores (20-25): Family relationships need boundaries

Low scores (5-10): You've established healthy dynamics

Generational Transmission (Questions 21-25)

High scores (20-25): Urgent need to break cycles

Low scores (5-10): You're already changing patterns

Update Readiness (Questions 26-30)

High scores (20-25): You're primed for transformation

Low scores (5-10): Consider building support first

What Your Score Means for Your Journey

Remember: This assessment is a starting point, not a verdict. Your score simply indicates where you are today. With each chapter of this book, with each week of practice, with each conscious choice, your algorithm updates.

Many readers find it helpful to retake this assessment after completing the 90-day transformation to see their progress. You might be surprised how much can change when you commit to updating your emotional algorithm.

Next Steps Based on Your Score

For All Scores:

Continue reading the book with your specific patterns in mind

Pay special attention to chapters that address your highest subscores

Consider finding an accountability partner for the journey

Be gentle with yourself—you're undertaking brave work

For Scores Above 90: Consider additional support through:

Professional therapy (especially IFS or narrative approaches)

Support groups for your specific patterns

The online community at GenerationalAlgorithm.com

Extra self-care during this transformation

A Final Note

You're not broken. You're not stuck. You're just running outdated software.

Time to update your emotional algorithm.

Return to Introduction or continue to Chapter 1

<APPENDIX_B>

THE 90-DAY TRANSFORMATION TRACKER
// Progress monitoring enabled...

Your Complete Journey Map

This tracker outlines your 12-week transformation journey. Each week builds on the previous one, corresponding to a chapter in the book.

How to Use: Read the chapter first, then choose 2-3 daily practices that resonate with you from the week's focus. You don't need to do everything—consistency with a few practices is better than overwhelming yourself.

MONTH ONE: DETECTION

Weeks 1-4: Learning to See the Patterns

Week 1: Algorithm Detection (Chapter 1)

Focus: Noticing your automatic emotional reactions

Key Question: "Is this my authentic response, or is this my programming?"

Core Practices:

Notice ONE automatic reaction daily

Track when you hear your parent's voice in your head

Celebrate any moment of awareness

Progress Check: ☐ I'm noticing patterns I couldn't see before

Week 2: Filter Awareness (Chapter 2)

Focus: Catching your interpretations and assumptions

Key Question: "What was actually said versus what did my filter add?"

Core Practices:

Catch yourself adding meaning to neutral comments

Ask an outsider's perspective once this week

Practice observing without interpreting

Progress Check: ☐ I can separate facts from my filter's additions

Week 3: Unmuting (Chapter 3)

Focus: Finding your emotional voice**Key Question:** "What would I express if I knew it was safe?"

Core Practices:

Journal one muted feeling daily

Practice one "I feel..." statement

Notice the urge to mute and pause

Progress Check: ☐ I expressed at least one difficult emotion

Week 4: Boundary Installation (Chapter 4)

Focus: Setting access controls

Key Question: "Is this person's access to me earned or assumed?"

Core Practices:

Identify ONE boundary to set

Practice it with a safe person first

Hold steady through any pushback

Progress Check: ☐ I set and maintained one new boundary

Month One Reflection: What patterns am I now aware of? ________________

MONTH TWO: UNDERSTANDING

Weeks 5-8: Exploring How Patterns Operate

Week 5: Switch-Flipping (Chapter 5)

Focus: Reclaiming your appropriate role

Key Question: "Am I responding as an adult, or as the parentified child?"

Core Practices:

Do something purely for fun

Let someone else handle their own problem

Practice saying "I don't know"

Progress Check: □ I allowed myself to not be responsible for everything

Week 6: Attachment Awareness (Chapter 6)

Focus: Understanding your connection patterns

Key Question: "Is this how I truly want to connect, or is this my attachment pattern?"

Core Practices:

Notice your attachment style activating

Try ONE opposite action

Share appropriate vulnerability

Progress Check: □ I recognized my attachment pattern in real-time

Week 7: Trauma Bond Break (Chapter 7)

Focus: Breaking toxic loops

Key Question: "Am I addicted to this person, or to the cycle?"

Core Practices:

Map ONE relationship cycle

Create a Reality Check Document

Practice not checking/engaging for set periods

Progress Check: ☐ I interrupted at least one toxic cycle

Week 8: Secret Assessment (Chapter 8)

Focus: Examining family archives

Key Question: "What family truth am I sensing but not speaking?"

Core Practices:

Notice topics your family avoids

Journal about sensed-but-unspoken truths

Share one personal truth safely

Progress Check: ☐ I acknowledged at least one family secret's impact

Month Two Reflection: What do I now understand about my patterns? ________________

MONTH THREE: TRANSFORMATION

Weeks 9-12: Creating Lasting Change

Week 9: Healing Exploration (Chapter 9)

Focus: Expanding your healing options

Key Question: "What part of me is afraid to try new healing methods?"

Core Practices:

Research ONE new healing modality

Try a 10-minute new practice

Notice resistance as information

Progress Check: □ I explored beyond my family's approved healing methods

Week 10: Update Installation (Chapter 10)

Focus: Beginning to rewrite patterns

Key Question: "What story am I ready to stop inheriting?"

Core Practices:

Choose ONE pattern to update

Practice new response 3x this week

Notice old pattern as "outdated software"

Progress Check: □ I successfully used a new response multiple times

Week 11: Reality Check (Chapter 11)

Focus: Dropping the performance

Key Question: "What would happen if we valued connection over impression?"

Core Practices:

Notice ONE family performance

Share an imperfection

Connect without documenting

Progress Check: □ I chose authenticity over image at least once

Week 12: Viral Healing (Chapter 12)

Focus: Spreading the medicine

Key Question: "How can my healing give others permission?"

Core Practices:

Share ONE healing win

Offer support to someone beginning their journey

Notice your ripple effects

Progress Check: □ I can see how my healing impacts others

Month Three Reflection: What transformations have taken root? ________________

YOUR 90-DAY SUMMARY

Three Major Insights:

Three Patterns Transformed:

My Next 90 Days:

Remember

Progress isn't linear

Small changes compound

Some weeks will be harder than others

You're rewriting generations of programming

Every moment of awareness counts

You don't have to be perfect. You just have to begin.

<APPENDIX_C>

THE COMPLETE DECODE TOOLKIT // Loading transformation tools...

Your Comprehensive Guide to Pattern Transformation

The DECODE method is your systematic approach to updating emotional algorithms. Use this toolkit repeatedly as you work through different inherited patterns.

Detect your inherited patterns

Examine the source code

Challenge outdated programming

Override with new responses

Download healthier patterns

Evolve your family legacy

DETECT: Becoming Aware

What It Is: Catching yourself running inherited patterns in real-time.

Key Practices:

Pattern Tracker - For one week, note:

Trigger → Your Response → How it felt familiar

Example: "Mom criticized → I shut down → Just like when I was 12"

Body Scan - Daily 5-minute check:

Where do you hold tension?

What emotion lives there?

When did this start?

Family Voice Journal - When you hear "should":

Write the exact words

Whose voice is speaking?

Is it still true today?

Core Question: "Where have I felt this before?"

EXAMINE: Understanding Origins

What It Is: Discovering when/why the pattern was installed and what purpose it served.

Key Practices:

Timeline Creation

First memory of pattern: _______

Who modeled it: _______

What it protected you from: _______

Cost-Benefit Analysis

Original Benefit	Current Cost
Kept me safe from...	Keeps me stuck in...

Three Generation Map

How grandparents expressed this

How parents modified it

How you carry it forward

Core Question: "What problem was this pattern originally solving?"

CHALLENGE: Question the Programming

What It Is: Testing whether old survival software still applies to current reality.

Key Practices:

Reality Check Questions

Is this still true in my life today?

Would I teach this to a child?

Who benefits from me keeping this pattern?

Exception Finder

List 3 times the pattern didn't activate

What was different?

What does this tell you?

Fear vs. Reality Chart

Pattern Says Will Happen	What Actually Happens
"They'll abandon me"	They expressed disappointment but stayed

Core Question: "Is this protecting me from current, real danger?"

OVERRIDE: Install New Responses

What It Is: Consciously choosing different responses when patterns activate.

Key Practices:

The Pause Protocol

STOP - Notice activation

BREATHE - Three deep breaths

CHOOSE - Select conscious response

ACT - Follow through

Opposite Action Plan

Old: Shut down in conflict → New: Express one feeling

Old: People-please → New: Consider your needs first

Old: Rage when triggered → New: Say "I need a moment"

Practice Schedule

Week 1-2: Safe people only

Week 3-4: Low stakes

Week 5-6: Medium challenge

Week 7-8: Family/high stakes

Core Question: "What would someone with healthy patterns do?"

DOWNLOAD: Integrate New Patterns

What It Is: Repeating new responses until they become your default setting.

Key Practices:

Success Library

Document each time you used new response

How it felt different

What improved

Daily Practice Menu (choose one)

Morning intention for new pattern

Midday check-in with yourself

Evening celebration of any progress

Weekly Integration Ritual

Review your Success Library

Notice what's becoming easier

Set intention for coming week

Core Question: "How can I reinforce this until it's automatic?"

EVOLVE: Create Generational Change

What It Is: Spreading healthy patterns to family and future generations.

Key Practices:

Model the Change

Let others witness your new responses

Share your journey when asked

Normalize growth and mistakes

Track the Ripples

Who's noticed your changes?

Who's asked for resources?

What family dynamics shifted?

Legacy Letter (write to future generations)

What pattern ended with you

Why you chose to change

What's now possible for them

Core Question: "How is my healing creating possibilities for others?"

Your DECODE Project Planner

Pattern I'm Working On: ____________________

My Timeline:

Week 1-2: Detect & Examine

Week 3-4: Challenge

Week 5-8: Override

Week 9-12: Download

Ongoing: Evolve

My Support Team:

Professional: __________

Personal: __________

Community: __________

Remember:

Start with your easiest pattern for practice

Progress isn't linear—expect setbacks

Small changes compound over time

You're rewriting generations of code

Be patient with yourself

The DECODE method isn't a one-time fix—it's a tool you'll use throughout your life as you discover and transform inherited patterns.

<APPENDIX_D>

EMERGENCY RESOURCES
// Critical support protocols...

When to Use This Section

This appendix is for moments when you need immediate help. If you're in crisis, skip to the section that applies to you. These resources are available 24/7. You don't have to handle this alone.

Remember: Seeking help is not weakness—it's wisdom. Your family patterns might say otherwise, but your life matters more than old programming.

IMMEDIATE CRISIS SUPPORT

If You're Thinking About Suicide

National Suicide Prevention Lifeline

Call or Text: 988 (24/7, free, confidential)

Chat online: 988lifeline.org

For Spanish: 1-888-628-9454

Crisis Text Line

Text HOME to 741741 (24/7, free)

For Spanish: Text AYUDA to 741741

International Crisis Lines

UK: 116 123 (Samaritans)

Australia: 13 11 14 (Lifeline)

Canada: 1-833-456-4566

Find your country: findahelpline.com

If You're Experiencing Domestic Violence

National Domestic Violence Hotline

Call: 1-800-799-7233 (24/7, free, confidential)

Text: START to 88788

Chat online: thehotline.org

TTY: 1-800-787-3224

Safety Planning: If you can't call safely:

Computer use can be monitored—use a safe device

Clear your browser history

Consider using a friend's phone

The Hotline can help create an escape plan

If You're Having a Mental Health Crisis

SAMHSA National Helpline

Call: 1-800-662-4357 (24/7, treatment referral and info)

Free, confidential, in English and Spanish

NAMI (National Alliance on Mental Illness)

Call: 1-800-950-NAMI (6264)

Monday-Friday, 10 AM-10 PM ET

Text NAMI to 741741 for crisis support

Email: helpline@nami.org

SPECIFIC SITUATION SUPPORT

Substance Use Crisis

SAMHSA National Helpline

1-800-662-4357 (24/7)

Treatment facility locator

Support for family members too

Crystal Meth Anonymous

1-855-638-4373

crystalmeth.org

Alcoholics Anonymous

aa.org (meeting finder)

Many offer online meetings

Child Abuse (Reporting or Support)

Childhelp National Child Abuse Hotline

1-800-422-4453 (24/7)

Professional crisis counselors

Interpretation in 170 languages

If a child is in immediate danger: Call 911

Sexual Assault Support

RAINN National Sexual Assault Hotline

1-800-656-4673 (24/7)

Chat online: online.rainn.org

Automatically routes to local services

LGBTQ+ Crisis Support

The Trevor Project (for youth under 25)

Call: 1-866-488-7386 (24/7)

Text: START to 678-678

Chat: thetrevorproject.org

LGBT National Hotline

1-888-843-4564

Monday-Friday 1 PM-9 PM PT

Youth hotline: 1-800-246-7743

Eating Disorder Crisis

National Eating Disorders Association

Call: 1-800-931-2237

Text: NEDA to 741741

Chat: nationaleatingdisorders.org

WHEN TO SEEK IMMEDIATE HELP

Go to the Emergency Room or Call 911 If:

Physical Danger:

Active thoughts of killing yourself with a plan

Thoughts of hurting others

Severe self-harm or injury

Overdose or poisoning

Severe withdrawal symptoms

Mental Health Emergencies:

Hearing voices telling you to hurt yourself/others

Severe paranoia or delusions

Complete disconnection from reality

Inability to care for yourself

Extreme agitation with risk of harm

Call a Crisis Line If:

Suicidal thoughts without immediate plan

Overwhelming emotional pain

Panic attacks that won't stop

Feeling completely alone

Need someone to talk to NOW

Unsure if you need emergency care

FINDING A THERAPIST (NON-EMERGENCY)

Therapy Directories

Psychology Today

psychologytoday.com/us/therapists

Filter by specialty, insurance, location

Read therapist profiles and approaches

For Postmodern/IFS Therapists:

IFS Institute: ifs-institute.com/practitioners

Narrative Therapy: dulwichcentre.com.au

Solution-Focused: sfbta.org

Specialized Directories:

BIPOC therapists: melaninandmentalhealth.com

LGBTQ+ affirming: glma.org

Lower cost: openpathcollective.org

Questions to Ask Potential Therapists

Are you familiar with family systems/generational trauma?

What's your experience with [your specific concern]?

Do you practice IFS or narrative therapy?

What's your approach to family patterns?

Do you offer sliding scale fees?

If You Can't Afford Therapy

Lower Cost Options:

Community mental health centers

University training clinics

Employee Assistance Programs (EAP)

Support groups (often free)

Online therapy platforms

Sliding scale therapists

Free Support Groups:

NAMI groups: nami.org/support

Adult Children of Alcoholics: adultchildren.org

SMART Recovery: smartrecovery.org

DailyStrength online groups: dailystrength.org

CREATING YOUR CRISIS PLAN

Before Crisis Hits:

1. Save These Numbers in Your Phone:

988 (Suicide Prevention)

Your therapist

Trusted friend/family

Local hospital

2. Write Down:

Warning signs you're struggling

What helps you feel safer

Coping strategies that work

Reasons to keep going

3. Remove Access:

Store medications safely

Remove or lock up weapons

Delete toxic contacts

Have someone hold credit cards if needed

4. Create a Safety Box:

Comfort items

Photos of loved ones

Encouraging letters

Favorite music/books

Self-soothing tools

FOR FAMILY MEMBERS

If Someone You Love Is in Crisis:

Do:

Take all threats seriously

Listen without judgment

Stay calm

Encourage professional help

Remove means of harm

Stay with them or ensure someone does

Don't:

Promise to keep secrets about safety

Try to solve everything yourself

Minimize their pain

Debate whether they should feel this way

Leave them alone if actively suicidal

Say:

"I'm here for you"

"You matter to me"

"Let's get through this together"

"I may not understand, but I care"

"Help is available"

Don't Say:

"You have so much to live for"

"Think how this affects me/family"

"You're being selfish"

"It's not that bad"

"Just think positive"

REMEMBER

Your family patterns might say:

"We don't air dirty laundry"

"Handle it yourself"

"Therapy is for weak people"

"What will people think?"

"You're overreacting"

But the truth is:

Your life matters more than family rules

Seeking help takes incredible strength

You deserve support and healing

Privacy isn't worth your life

Your feelings are valid

You are not alone. Help is available. Recovery is possible.

Even if your family never modeled help-seeking, you can be the first. Even if generations suffered in silence, you could choose differently. Your healing journey might start with a crisis, but it doesn't have to end there.

This is not the end of your story. It's the beginning of your transformation.

Keep this appendix somewhere accessible. Share it with others who might need it. Remember: Breaking generational patterns sometimes means being the first to say, "I need help."

<REFERENCES>

SYSTEM DOCUMENTATION

// Source files and dependencies...

> Accessing library: trauma_healing_research.db > Files found: 127

> Loading citations...

Introduction

- Schore, A. N. (2019). *Right brain psychotherapy*. W. W. Norton & Company.
- Siegel, D. J. (2020). *The developing mind: How relationships and the brain interact to shape who we are* (3rd ed.). Guilford Press.

Chapter 1: Your Personalized Emotional Feed

- Perry, B. D., & Winfrey, O. (2021). *What happened to you?: Conversations on trauma, resilience, and healing*. Flatiron Books.
- Schore, A. N. (2003). *Affect regulation and the repair of the self*. W. W. Norton & Company.
- van der Kolk, B. (2014). *The body keeps the score: Brain, mind, and body in the healing of trauma*. Penguin Books.

Chapter 2: Filtered Reality

- Kahneman, D. (2011). *Thinking, fast and slow*. Farrar, Straus and Giroux.
- Siegel, D. J. (2010). *Mindsight: The new science of personal transformation*. Bantam Books.

Chapter 3: Muted Emotions

- Gross, J. J. (2002). Emotion regulation: Affective, cognitive, and social consequences. *Psychophysiology*, 39(3), 281-291.
- Gross, J. J., & John, O. P. (2003). Individual differences in two emotion regulation processes: Implications for affect, relationships, and well-being. *Journal of Personality and Social Psychology*, 85(2), 348-362.

Chapter 4: Blocked and Unfriended

- Felitti, V. J., Anda, R. F., Nordenberg, D., Williamson, D. F., Spitz, A. M., Edwards, V., ... & Marks, J. S. (1998). Relationship of childhood abuse and household dysfunction to many of the leading causes of death in adults: The Adverse Childhood Experiences (ACE) Study. *American Journal of Preventive Medicine*, 14(4), 245-258.

Chapter 5: Flip the Switch—Reversed Roles and Parentification

- Hooper, L. M. (2007). The application of attachment theory and family systems theory to the phenomena of parentification. *The Family Journal*, 15(3), 217-223.

- Perry, B. D. (2006). *The boy who was raised as a dog: And other stories from a child psychiatrist's notebook*. Basic Books.

Chapter 6: Follow, Unfollow—Attachment Patterns in the Family

- Bowlby, J. (1988). *A secure base: Parent-child attachment and healthy human development*. Basic Books.
- Levine, A., & Heller, R. (2010). *Attached: The new science of adult attachment and how it can help you find—and keep—love*. TarcherPerigee.
- Main, M., & Solomon, J. (1986). Discovery of an insecure-disorganized/disoriented attachment pattern. In T. B. Brazelton & M. W. Yogman (Eds.), *Affective development in infancy* (pp. 95-124). Ablex Publishing.

Chapter 7: Stuck in the Loop—Trauma Bonding and Engagement Cycles

- Carnes, P. (1997). *The betrayal bond: Breaking free of exploitive relationships*. Health Communications, Inc.
- Fisher, H. (2004). *Why we love: The nature and chemistry of romantic love*. Henry Holt and Company.
- Herman, J. L. (2015). *Trauma and recovery: The aftermath of violence—from domestic abuse to political terror*. Basic Books.

Chapter 8: The Archive of Secrets—Unarchiving Family History

- Bradshaw, J. (2005). *Family secrets: The path to self-acceptance and reunion*. Bantam Books.

- Imber-Black, E. (1999). *The secret life of families: Making decisions about secrets: When keeping secrets can harm you, when keeping secrets can heal you—and how to know the difference*. Bantam Books.
- van der Kolk, B. A. (2014). *The body keeps the score: Brain, mind, and body in the healing of trauma*. Viking.

Chapter 9: The Explore Page of Healing—Seeking New Inputs and Perspectives

- Maté, G. (2003). *When the body says no: The cost of hidden stress*. Vintage Canada.
- Shapiro, F. (2001). *Eye movement desensitization and reprocessing (EMDR): Basic principles, protocols, and procedures* (2nd ed.). Guilford Press.
- Wampold, B. E. (2015). How important are the common factors in psychotherapy? An update. *World Psychiatry*, 14(3), 270-277.

Chapter 10: Algorithm Update—Rewriting the Code for the Next Generation

- Cozolino, L. (2017). *The neuroscience of psychotherapy: Healing the social brain* (3rd ed.). W. W. Norton & Company.
- Doidge, N. (2007). *The brain that changes itself: Stories of personal triumph from the frontiers of brain science*. Penguin Books.
- Hanson, R. (2013). *Hardwiring happiness: The new brain science of contentment, calm, and confidence*. Harmony Books.

Chapter 11: The Highlight Reel vs. Reality—Breaking the Facade of Family "Perfection"

- Brown, B. (2012). *Daring greatly: How the courage to be vulnerable transforms the way we live, love, parent, and lead*. Gotham Books.

- Vaillant, G. E. (2012). *Triumphs of experience: The men of the Harvard Grant Study*. Belknap Press.
- Waldinger, R. J., & Schulz, M. S. (2023). *The good life: Lessons from the world's longest scientific study of happiness*. Simon & Schuster.

Chapter 12: Going Viral for Good—Spreading Healing, Not Trauma

- Christakis, N. A., & Fowler, J. H. (2009). *Connected: The surprising power of our social networks and how they shape our lives*. Little, Brown and Company.
- Christakis, N. A., & Fowler, J. H. (2013). Social contagion theory: Examining dynamic social networks and human behavior. *Statistics in Medicine*, 32(4), 556-577.
- Pentland, A. (2014). *Social physics: How good ideas spread—the lessons from a new science*. Penguin Press.

Additional Core References

Trauma and Healing

- Herman, J. L. (1992). *Trauma and recovery*. Basic Books.
- Levine, P. A. (1997). *Waking the tiger: Healing trauma*. North Atlantic Books.
- Ogden, P., Minton, K., & Pain, C. (2006). *Trauma and the body: A sensorimotor approach to psychotherapy*. W. W. Norton & Company.
- Rothschild, B. (2000). *The body remembers: The psychophysiology of trauma and trauma treatment*. W. W. Norton & Company.

Family Systems

- Bowen, M. (1978). *Family therapy in clinical practice.* Jason Aronson.
- McGoldrick, M., Gerson, R., & Petry, S. (2008). *Genograms: Assessment and intervention* (3rd ed.). W. W. Norton & Company.
- Minuchin, S. (1974). *Families and family therapy.* Harvard University Press.

Neuroscience and Neuroplasticity

- Davidson, R. J., & Begley, S. (2012). *The emotional life of your brain.* Hudson Street Press.
- LeDoux, J. (2015). *Anxious: Using the brain to understand and treat fear and anxiety.* Viking.
- Porges, S. W. (2011). *The polyvagal theory: Neurophysiological foundations of emotions, attachment, communication, and self-regulation.* W. W. Norton & Company.
- Siegel, D. J. (2012). *The developing mind: How relationships and the brain interact to shape who we are* (2nd ed.). Guilford Press.

Addiction and Recovery

- Beattie, M. (1992). *Codependent no more: How to stop controlling others and start caring for yourself.* Hazelden Publishing.
- Black, C. (2001). *It will never happen to me: Growing up with addiction as youngsters, adolescents, adults.* Hazelden Publishing.
- Woititz, J. G. (1983). *Adult children of alcoholics.* Health Communications, Inc.

Attachment Theory

- Ainsworth, M. D. S., Blehar, M. C., Waters, E., & Wall, S. (1978). *Patterns of attachment: A psychological study of the strange situation.* Lawrence Erlbaum Associates.
- Main, M. (2000). The organized categories of infant, child, and adult attachment: Flexible vs. inflexible attention under attachment-related stress. *Journal of the American Psychoanalytic Association*, 48(4), 1055-1096.
- Sroufe, L. A. (2005). Attachment and development: A prospective, longitudinal study from birth to adulthood. *Attachment & Human Development*, 7(4), 349-367.

Epigenetics and Intergenerational Trauma

- Bowers, M. E., & Yehuda, R. (2016). Intergenerational transmission of stress in humans. *Neuropsychopharmacology*, 41(1), 232-244.
- Yehuda, R., & Lehrner, A. (2018). Intergenerational transmission of trauma effects: Putative role of epigenetic mechanisms. *World Psychiatry*, 17(3), 243-257.

Cultural and Social Perspectives

- hooks, b. (2004). *The will to change: Men, masculinity, and love.* Washington Square Press.
- Sue, D. W., & Sue, D. (2012). *Counseling the culturally diverse: Theory and practice* (6th ed.). John Wiley & Sons.

Popular Psychology and Self-Help

- Brown, B. (2010). *The gifts of imperfection.* Hazelden Publishing.

- Gibson, L. C. (2015). *Adult children of emotionally immature parents*. New Harbinger Publications.
- Walker, P. (2013). *Complex PTSD: From surviving to thriving*. Azure Coyote Publishing.
- Wolynn, M. (2016). *It didn't start with you: How inherited family trauma shapes who we are and how to end the cycle*. Viking.

Research Methodology

- American Psychological Association. (2020). *Publication manual of the American Psychological Association* (7th ed.). American Psychological Association.
- Creswell, J. W., & Creswell, J. D. (2018). *Research design: Qualitative, quantitative, and mixed methods approaches* (5th ed.). SAGE Publications.

Note on Statistics and Research

Many statistics cited throughout this book are composites drawn from multiple studies or represent clinical observations rather than single research findings. The field of intergenerational trauma and family systems is rapidly evolving, and readers are encouraged to explore current research for the most up-to-date findings.

Additional Resources

For the most current research on trauma, family systems, and healing:

- International Society for Traumatic Stress Studies (ISTSS)
- American Psychological Association (APA)
- National Institute of Mental Health (NIMH)

- Substance Abuse and Mental Health Services Administration (SAMHSA)
- The National Child Traumatic Stress Network (NCTSN)

Note: This reference list includes both actual published works and representative citations for the types of research mentioned in the book. Readers should verify specific statistics and findings with current peer-reviewed sources.

Made in the USA
Monee, IL
24 August 2025

22817376R00094